The Ultimate
NINJA FOODI
COOKBOOK

800 Effortless Foolproof Recipes to Air Fry, Pressure Cook, Dehydrate and more

By
Alexander Peterson

DISCLAIMER

The information contained in this book is geared for educational and entertainment purposes only. Strenuous efforts have been made towards providing accurate, up to date and reliable complete information. The information in this book is true and complete to the best of our knowledge. Neither the publisher nor the author takes

any responsibility for any possible consequences of reading or enjoying the recipes in

this book. The author and publisher disclaim any liability in connection with the use of information contained in this book. Under no circumstance will any legal responsibility or blame be apportioned against the author or publisher for any reparation, damages, or monetary loss due to the information herein, either directly or indirectly.

Table of Contents

CHAPTER 1: INTRODUCTION

Benefits of Using the Ninja Foodi:

There are lots of benefits you can get from using this appliance. The benefit that outweighs other appliances is that it does not require you to flip the fries over to the other side many times compared to other pressure cookers. You may only shake the fries on halfway to cooking time for a proper cooking. The benefits are shown below:

1. **Crispy Wings**

Start cooking your chicken or turkey wings even in haste with the pressure cooker mode. When the normal cooking is done, switch to the air fryer to get that hot air circulating all around the wings and gives you a crispy result. You can combine with any sauce of your choice for your dinner or as an appetizer.

2. **Baked Macaroni and Cheese**

This unit allows you to cook macaroni and cheese and gives you a crispy result. When you are done with the normal cooking, you can swap to the Air Fryer mode for that crispy golden-brown topping that you would get when baked.

3. **Scalloped Potatoes**

Everybody loves a eating creamy scalloped potatoes. The unit tenders your potatoes and then with the air fryer for a crispy result. Ninja Foodi allows you to cook all kinds of food unlike other units like air fryer or pressure cooker.

4. **Pressure cook and crisp**

Ninja Foodi enables you to pressure cook something and then make it crispy. This crispiness makes the chicken you cook not to require that you bring the chicken to the broiler. Everything can stay neat and nice.

Cooking things at once is very beneficial and helpful to Ninja Foodi users because it is not time-consuming cooking a healthy food with the unit. The parts are easy to clean and it has a large cooking capacity.

Function Keys of Your Ninja Foodi:

Ninja Foodi comes with many buttons for optimum operation of the unit which includes steam, slow cook, pressure cook, sear/sauté button, air crisp, broil, bake /roast and keep warm, buttons respectively. It also has buttons for temperature and time controls, start/stop button. The buttons and their functions are shown below:

1. **Pressure cook:**

This button helps you to cook your meal up to 4 hours using high or low pressure. As earlier said, it is possible to adjust the cooking time to 1-minute increment for 1 hour. When the time is up, you may increase the time to 5 minutes and begin to cook up to 4 hours. Hence you can make a whole lot of meals.

2. **Air Crisp:**

This function gives you an opportunity to adjust the temperature to either 300°F or 400°F and also adjust to increase the cooking time to 2 minutes for the highest cooking time of 1 hour. The air crisp button is used in cooking many dishes like chicken tenders, French fries etc. Pressure cooked food can be crisp using this button.

3. **Bake/Roast:**

This setting in the Ninja is good for making roasted meats and baked foods. For this function, the Ninja Foodi uses the air-frying lid. There is no problem if you set the cooking time to 1-minute increment for 1 hour. When the time is up, you may increase the time to 5 minutes and begin to cook up to 4 hours. After the hour mark, you can increase the time in five-minute increments and cook for up to four hours.

4. **Steam:**

It is possible to steam your veggies and other meals by putting the pressure lid on the Ninja Foodi with the sealing valve in the vent position.

5. **Slow cook:**

This button also makes use of the pressure lid with the sealing valve in the vent position. It is possible for you to slow cook low or slow cook high. The cooking time can also be adjusted to 15 minutes increment for up to 12 hours. It is advisable to use the slow cook mode when cooking meals like stews, soup or pot roasts.

6. **Sear/Sauté:**

This button on the Ninja Foodi does not make use of the lid. It only has a temperature setting of 5 different modes respectively. These includes: medium, medium-high, high, low or medium-low, setting. Foods can be browned after cooking or before cooking. The button can also be used to make different kinds of sauces, gravies. This button functions the same as you would sear or sauté using your stovetop.

Steps on How to Use Your Ninja Foodi:

This appliance is a very friendly and easy-to-use kitchen unit.

For Ninja Foodi pressure cooker:

1. Always put your foods in the inner pot of the Ninja Foodi or you put your food in the Air Fryer basket. This is basically good for meats.

2. Press the power on function.

3. Close lid in place. Do not put the one that is attached.

4. Set the top steam valve to seal position and press the pressure function.

5. Adjust the temperature to either high or low using the + or − buttons respectively.

6. Set the cooking time using the + or − buttons.

7. Press Start button.

8. The Ninja Foodi will take a little time to reach pressure and then will count the number of minutes until it reaches zero minute.

For Ninja Foodi Air Fryer:

1. Make use of the lid that is attached.

2. Place the Air Fryer cooking basket inside the Ninja Foodi inner pot.

3. Place your food inside the cooking basket.

4. Lock the attached lid and switch on the Ninja Foodi by pressing the button at the bottom.

5. Push the air crisp button.

6. Select the temperature you want to use by pressing the + and − buttons.

7. Set the cooking time by pressing the + and − buttons.

8. Select start button.

Useful Tips & Tricks for Using Your Ninja Foodi

It is pertinent to inquire to know how to properly use a new appliance you bought. Ninja Foodi come with 2 distinct lids. One is for the electric pressure cooker while the other one is for the Air Fryer lid. It is possible to use both lids in on food. Immediately the pressure cooker is done, remove the pressure cooker lid and put the Air Fryer lid. This helps to crisp your food. Every new kitchen appliance you get comes with an operational manual to guide you on the proper usage of the unit. Below are some few tips for the proper usage of your Ninja Foodi:

1. Whenever you want to spray cooking spray on the inner pot of your Ninja Foodi, do not use aerosol cooking spray.

2. Try to use the recommended amount of water or broth if you are using the pressure-cooking button. Wrong usage of water may not give you the desired result.

3. When you are not using your Ninja Foodi, unplug from any power source so as to avoid the appliance switch on by itself even when you did not press the power on button.

4. It is not advisable to use your Ninja Foodi on your stove top. This can easily damage the unit.

Ninja Foodi Troubleshooting Tips

Every electronic appliance sometimes has trouble shooting or shows a faulty message on the display. Below are some of the major trouble shooting or problems you could find on your Ninja Foodi.

1. My appliance is taking a long time to come to pressure. Why?

It is important to know how long it takes your Ninja Foodi to come to pressure. Base on a particular temperature you choose, cooking time may vary. Temperature of the cooking pot at the moment of cooking including the amount of ingredients also makes cooking time to vary. If the cooking time is taking a longer time than necessary, make sure your silicone ring is fully seated and flush against the lid, make sure the pressure lid is fully closed and set the pressure release valve to seal position.

2. Why is the cooking time counting slowly?

You have to make sure you set the time correctly. Check if you did not use hours instead of minutes. Note that the HH stands for hours while the MM stands for minutes on the display window respectively. You can increase or decrease the cooking time.

3. How do I know when the appliance is pressurizing?

When the appliance is building pressure, the rotating lights will display on the display window. When you are using steam or pressure mode, light will rotate on the display screen. It means the appliance is preheating. Immediately the preheating process finishes, the normal cooking time starts counting.

4. When I'm using the steam mode, my unit is bringing out a lot of steam.

During cooking, steam releasing on the pressure release valve is normal. It is advisable to allow the pressure release valve in the vent position for Steam, Slow Cook, and Sear or Sauté mode.

5. Why can't I take off the pressure lid?

The Ninja Foodi has to be depressurized before the pressure lid can be opened. This is one of the safety measures put by the manufacturer. In order to do a quick pressure release, set the pressure release valve to the vent position. Immediately the pressure is released completely, the lid will be ready to open.

6. Do I need to lose the pressure release valve?

The answer is yes. You have to loosen the pressure release valve. It helps to circulate pressure through some release of small amount of steam while cooking is done for the result to be excellent.

Ninja Foodi Frequently Asked Questions and Answers:

Question 1: Can I deep fry chicken with this appliance?

Answer: Yes, it is possible. You can cook a chicken in your Ninja Foodi. This is a new modern way of cooking that can tender your food and progress to crisping the food using hot air and give you a crispy result.

Question 2: Can I Take My Ninja Pot from the Refrigerator and Put directly in the appliance?

Answer: Yes, you can do it if your pot was in the refrigerator.

Question 3: Can the Pot enter under the Broiler or the Oven?

Answer: Yes. It is possible but you have to be extra careful while putting or taking the pot out from the Ninja Foodi. It is only the lid that you do not need to put under the oven or the broiler.

Question 4: Can the Baking or cooking pan enter under the oven?

Answer: Yes. It is very possible and good to put the cooking pan under the oven. You just need to be careful while inserting the pan.

Question 5: Can I use the buffet settings to cook?

Answer: NO. It is not advisable to do that because the buffet function is just to keep temperature that is above 140°F when the food has been cooked to 165°F.

Question 6: What is the meaning of One-pot Meal Cooking?

Answer: These are important family meal that could be ready within 30 minutes time. The one pot helps in a quick clean up.

Question 7: What differentiate model op301 from model op305?

Answer: Model OP305 has the Dehydrate button while model OP301 has no dehydrate button. That's the major difference.

Question 8: Can you can food with Ninja Foodi?

Answer: No, you will not be able to can food with this appliance. You can only do it if you have a pressure canner can.

Question 9: Why is the time beeper not beeping?

Answer: You can check the volume level.

Question 10: Can I put frozen pork loin in my Ninja Foodi?

Answer: Yes. It is possible to do that. Frozen foods can be cooked with this appliance.

Question 11: If the Ninja foodi displays water, what is the meaning?

Answer: It means that you need to put more water into the Ninja Foodi. If at a point of putting more water and the error still show up, contact the customer care on 877581-7375.

Question 12: Can meat and cheese vegetables be cooked with this appliance?

Answer: No. Ninja Foodi was not meant for canning of foods. So, it will not work for you.

Ninja Foodi Pressure Releasing Methods:

This process is ideal for stopping all cooking process in order to avoid the food getting burnt. Foods like corn or broccoli etc. are ideal for this pressure releasing. There are two types of pressure release namely: Quick and natural pressure release.

1. **How to do a Ninja Foodi Quick Release**

Immediately the cooking time is up, keep the venting knob on Venting Position to enable Ninja Foodi quickly release the pressure inside the pressure cooker. To release all the pressure, it normally takes some few minutes. Before you open the lid, wait until the valve drops.

2. **How to do a Ninja Foodi Natural Release**

Immediately the cooking time is up, you have to wait until the valve drops and the lid is opened. In order to make sure all the pressure is released before opening the lid, keep the venting knob on Venting Position. This particular pressure release technique normally takes about 10 – 25 minutes but it depends on the amount of food in your cooker. To do the 10 – 15 minutes pressure release, when the cooking time is up, wait 10 – 15 minutes before moving the Venting Knob from Sealing Position to Venting Position so as to enable the remaining pressure to be released. Do not fail to wait for the floating valve to drop before you open the lid.

BREAKFAST RECIPE

Apple Cinnamon Oatmeal

Preparation time: 5 minutes

Cooking time: 25 minutes

Overall time: 30 minutes

Serves: 2 to 4 people

Recipe Ingredients:

- 1 cup of steel oats
- 1 teaspoon of cinnamon
- 1 each Apple, cored, peeled and diced
- 4 cups of water

Cooking Instructions:

1. Core, peel and dice apple, add oats, apple and cinnamon to your Ninja Foodi.

2. Add water to the Ninja Foodi and stir well. Close pressure lid and set to high mode for about 10 minutes.

3. Let pressure naturally release for about 15 minutes once complete. Cooked oatmeal.

4. Open lid and stir oatmeal. It is very hot, but as you place in bowls add sweetener such as brown sugar, or honey.

5. Add any other toppings desired such as raisins or nuts. Serve immediately and Enjoy!

Mushroom Tofu Ramen

Preparation time: 5 minutes

Cooking time: 30 minutes

Overall time: 35 minutes

Serves: 2 to 4 people

Recipe Ingredients:

- Tofu
- 1 (16 ounces) of block extra firm tofu
- 2 tablespoons of olive oil
- Salt
- Pepper
- Ramen
- 4 cups of miso Ginger Broth
- 2 cloves of garlic, crushed
- 8 ounces of baby bella mushrooms, sliced
- 1 (1 ounces) package of dried Shitake mushrooms
- 2 cups of water
- 1 package of Ramen Noodles, flavor packet discarded
- ¼ cup of green onion
- 2 Japanese Marinated Soft Boiled Eggs (optional)
- Black sesame seeds, for garnish (optional)

Cooking Instructions:

1. Press the tofu to release any excess water Slice tofu into 1 -inch cubes. In a medium sized bowl, toss the tofu cubes in olive oil and season with salt and pepper.

2. Turn Ninja Foodie on "Air Crisp" to the function, preheat for about 5 minutes at 400°F, spray the crisper basket with non-stick spray.

3. Place tofu in the basket, "crisp" for 15 minutes, tossing the tofu every 5 minutes so it crisps evenly.

4. When tofu is done, remove the basket and set it aside. Switch the Ninja Foodie to the Pressure function.

5. Pour the miso ginger broth into the pot, add the garlic and mushroom and seal the pot with the pressure cook lid, make sure the pressure valve is set to seal position.

6. Cook for about 10 minutes at high pressure. You can release pressure quickly or slowly. When it is safe to do so, open the lid and add 2 cups of water.

7. Switch to the Sear/Sauté function, liquid will quickly come to a boil. Add the Ramen Noodles, cook for about 3 minutes.

8. Carefully remove the pot from the Ninja Foodi and divide the broth and noodles into 2 large soup bowls.

9. Top each with a generous amount of tofu, green onions, 1 halved Japanese Marinated Soft Boiled Egg and a sprinkle of black sesame seeds.

10. Serve immediately and Enjoy immediately!

Scrambled Eggs

Preparation time: 3 minutes

Cooking time: 9 minutes

Overall time: 12 minutes

Serves: 2 to 4 people

Recipe Ingredients:

- 1/3 tbsp. of unsalted butter
- 2 eggs
- 2 tbsp. of milk
- Salt and pepper to taste
- 1/8 cup of cheddar cheese

Cooking Instructions:

1. Place butter in an air fryer-safe pan and place inside the ninja foodi.

2. Cook at 300°F until butter is melted, for about 2 minutes. Whisk together the eggs and milk, then add salt and pepper to taste.

3. Place eggs in pan and cook it on 300°F for about 3 minutes, then push eggs to the inside of the pan to stir them around.

4. Cook for 2 more minutes then add cheddar cheese, stirring the eggs again. Cook 2 more minutes.

5. Remove pan from the air fryer and enjoy them immediately.

Crispy Bacon

Preparation time: 5 minutes

Cooking time: 10 minutes

Overall time: 15 minutes

Serves: 4 to 6 people

Recipe Ingredients:

- Package of Bacon, 12 ounces

Cooking Instructions:

1. Prepare the air fryer by adding a piece of uncooked bread underneath the air fryer basket, but inside the pressure cooker basket.

2. After you have prepped the Ninja Foodi, peel each pieces of bacon from the package and using tongs, place in piles into the air fryer basket.

3. You can add approximately 12 to 14 slices of bacon, it is fine if the bacon overlaps and touches other pieces.

4. Close air fryer lid and set your Ninja Foodi to Air crisp, 390°F and set time to 11 minutes.

5. Press the start button, at the 5-minute mark, open the foodi with tongs, rearrange the bacon.

6. It won't be done yet. Close the lid and let continue cooking. Around the 9-minute mark, check the bacon for Your level of doneness.

7. Remember the bacon is hot and will continue to cook just a tad even after removal from the basket, crisping up to the final level on a plate in a minute or two.

8. Serve immediately and Enjoy!

Egg and Avocado

Preparation time: 5 minutes

Cooking time: 10 minutes

Overall time: 15 minutes

Serves: 2 to 4 people

Recipe Ingredients:

- 1 Avocado
- Salt and Pepper to taste
- Cooking spray and tin foil
- 2 eggs

Cooking Instructions:

1. Cut avocado in half, scoop some out and place a cracked egg in each half of the avocado.

2. Add salt and pepper to taste Top with cheese Place on sprayed foil squares and place into air fry basket.

3. Air crisp at 390ºF for about 10 to 12 minutes. Serve immediately and Enjoy!

Cheesy Flatbread

Preparation time: 10 minutes

Cooking time: 8 minutes

Overall time 18 minutes

Recipe Ingredients:

- 1 tube of pizza dough
- ½ cup of butter
- 1 teaspoon of garlic
- A sprinkle of dried or fresh parsley and dried Italian seasoning
- 2 cups of Mozza cheese, shredded
- Other preferred toppings

Cooking Instructions:

1. Open and unroll the pizza dough, check for cracks or holes in the dough.

2. Reroll the dough, rolling it on the long side Cut 1" rolls and then flatten and roll them out to approximately 6" diameter Mix the butter, garlic, and herbs together.

3. Brush over the top of the dough. Place them on the Foodi rack and air crisp the dough for about 4 minutes or until it becomes golden brown.

4. Flip, brush the dough again with the butter and do the air fry till golden for the other side.

5. Sprinkle some of the cheese over the top of the bread and air fry until the cheese melts Add any extra toppings but watch that they don't burn.

6. Serve immediately and Enjoy!

Hashbrown casserole

Preparation time: 5 minutes

Cooking time: 30 minutes

Overall time: 35 minutes

Serves: 8 to 10 people

Recipe Ingredients:

- 6 eggs
- 48 ounces of bag frozen hashbrowns
- ¼ cup of milk
- 1 large onion
- 3 tablespoons of olive oil
- 1 lb. of Ham
- ½ cup of cheddar cheese

Cooking Instructions:

1. Turn your Foodi on Sauté mode and add olive oil and chopped onion cook on sauté till translucent.

2. Add in frozen hashbrowns and turn on Air Crips 350°F for about 15 minutes Flipping half way through the cooking time.

3. Mix together eggs and milk and pour over your golden hashbrowns and add your breakfast meat.

4. Add your meat to the top Place Foodi on Air crisp 350°F for about 10 minutes or until top is golden brown and eggs are done.

5. Top with Cheddar cheese and close lid till cheese melts about 1 minute

Air Crispy Bacon

Preparation time: 5 minutes

Cooking time 10 minutes

Overall time 15 minutes

Serves: 4 to 6 people

Recipe Ingredients:

- 1 pound of bacon

Cooking Instructions:

1. Add 4 to 5 strips of bacon to the air fryer basket of your Ninja Foodi. Close the lid then press Start.

2. Press Air Crisp then set the temperature to 400°F using the arrow buttons. Then set the time to 10 minutes using the arrow buttons.

3. Press Start and the time will begin to count down. Be sure to flip the bacon halfway through cooking with the tongs.

4. Once the bacon is cooked to your desired crispiness, place the cooked bacon on a large plate lined with paper towels and let cool.

5. Serve immediately and Enjoy!

Breakfast Burritos

Preparation time: 10 minutes

Cooking time: 45 minutes

Overall time: 55 minutes

Serves: 2 to 4 people

Recipe Ingredients:

- 1 teaspoon of olive oil
- 1 pound of breakfast sausage
- 1 medium russet potato about 2 cups
- 2 teaspoons of sea salt divided
- 1 teaspoon of black pepper divided
- 10 large eggs
- 3 cups of cheese shredded
- 12 (8") flour tortillas

Cooking Instructions:

1. Cut and dice your medium sized Russet potato into ½ inch dice. Soak your diced potatoes in cold water for at least 30 minutes.

2. Add 1 teaspoon of olive oil to the inner pot of the Ninja Foodi and turn the sauté mode to high.

3. Add in 1 pound of breakfast sausage and sauté the sausage until it is about 1/2 way cooked and the fat begins to render out.

4. It will take about 5 to 7 minutes. Add the diced and drained potatoes, along with 1 tsp salt and ½ teaspoon of pepper.

5. Sauté just until you can easily pierce the potato, but it is still firm. It takes about 5 to 7 minutes.

6. While the potatoes and sausage are sautéing, lightly scramble your eggs with 1 tsp salt and ½ teaspoon of pepper.

7. Move the potatoes and sausage around so they cover the entire bottom of the inner pot of the Ninja Foodi. Pour in the scrambled eggs and turn off the Sauté mode.

8. Cover the Inner Pot with aluminum foil and punch at least 10 small holes in the top to allow some air flow, but not the full force of the fan.

9. Select the Bake function and set the temp to 325°F and the time for about 20 minutes.

10. After 15 minutes, remove the foil and allow to bake the remaining 5 minutes. Remove burrito filling from the inner pot and place into a mixing bowl.

11. Place the rack or basket into the Ninja Foodi and set the Air Crisp to 375°F to pre-heat. Assemble your breakfast burrito.

12. Add ½ cup of filling onto one side of the tortilla shell and top with about 1 to 2 tablespoons of shredded cheese.

13. Brush with olive oil or butter. Place up to 4 burritos seam side down onto the rack or in the basket of the Ninja Foodi.

14. Air Crisp at 375°F for 10 minutes, flipping half way through. Serve immediately and Enjoy!

Egg Bites

Preparation time: 5 minutes

Cooking time: 8 minutes

Overall time: 20 minutes

Serves: 5 to 7 people

Recipe Ingredients:

- 4 large eggs
- ¼ cup of cottage cheese
- 1/2 cup shredded cheese
- 3 strips of cooked bacon- cut into bite sized pieces
- ¼ cup of heavy whipping cream
- ¼ tsp. of salt
- Non-stick cooking spray
- Pepper to taste (about 1/4 teaspoon if desired)

Cooking Instructions:

1. Beat eggs, cream, cottage cheese, salt and pepper together until evenly combined. Lightly spray silicone egg bites mold with non-stick cooking spray.

2. Fill egg bites mold ½ of the way full with egg mixture. Add a tablespoon of shredded cheese to each egg mold.

3. Add about ½ piece of cooked bacon to each egg mold. Make sure that you do not overflow the egg bite mold with the ingredients.

4. Gently stir each egg mold until ingredients are well combined. Cover filled egg bites mold with foil. Pour 1 cup of water into the Ninja Foodi insert pot.

5. Place a trivet into the Ninja Foodi and lower your filled egg bites mold onto the trivet. Close pressure-cooking lid and move valve to "seal" position.

6. Turn Ninja Foodi On and choose pressure cooker setting. Choose "low" and change time to 8 minutes. Push the start button.

7. When timer beeps, let pressure naturally release for about 5 minutes and then quick release remaining pressure.

8. Open pressure cooker lid and remove egg bites from Ninja Foodi. Remove foil and let cool for about 2 minutes.

9. Place a plate on top of egg bites and flip the egg bites onto the plate. Remove foil and let it cool for about 2 minutes.

10. Place a plate on top of egg bites and flip the egg bites onto the plate. Serve immediately and Enjoy!

Cracked Out Tater Tot Breakfast Casserole

Preparation time: 15 minutes

Cooking time: 30 minutes

Overall time: 45 minutes

Serves: 2 to 4 people

Recipe Ingredients:

- 1 pound of bacon
- ½ bag of frozen tater tots, 32 ounces
- 1 cup of shredded cheddar cheese
- 4 eggs
- 1 cups of milk
- ½ package of Ranch dressing mix

Cooking Instructions:

1. Cook Bacon, place in crisp basket and close the crisping lid.

2. Select Air Crisp, set temp to 390 degrees and set time to 12 minutes. Select Start. Start checking your bacon after about 6 minutes.

3. You will want to move it around with a fork to keep it crisping evenly and to prevent to pieces from sticking together.

4. Once cooked to your desired crispness, set aside in paper towels to get the grease off.

5. In a large bowl, mix tator tots, bacon & cheese. Whisk eggs, milk & ranch dressing. Pour over tator tots and mix to combine.

6. Spray pot with canola spray. Pour tator tot mixture into your pot. Close crisping lid. Select Air Crisp, set temp to 350 degrees and set time to 25 min.

7. Select Start. check your casserole after about 15 minutes. Serve immediately and Enjoy!

Mac and Cheese with Bacon

Preparation time: 5 minutes

Cooking time: 15 minutes

Overall time: 20 minutes

Serves: 8 to 10 minutes

Recipe Ingredients:

- 8 ounces of banza Pasta Elbows
- 2 slices of Bacon, cut into strips
- 4 cloves of (15g) Garlic, minced
- 2 cups (480ml) of chicken Broth
- 1 cups (240ml) of unsweetened almond milk
- 6 ounces of freshly shredded cheddar cheese, divided
- 1 ounces of freshly shredded parmesan

Optional Seasoning:

- 1 teaspoon of dry mustard
- 1 teaspoon parsley flakes
- ½ teaspoon of black pepper
- ¼ teaspoon of ground nutmeg
- ¼ teaspoon of salt, to taste

Cooking Instructions:

1. Use the Ninja Foodi's sauté function to fully cook the bacon.

2. Once cooked, transfer the cooked bacon to a paper towel. Turn off the Foodi and add the garlic to the remaining bacon grease.

3. Cook until the garlic starts to turn golden brown, about 30 seconds, before adding the chicken broth.

4. Add the uncooked pasta to the broth and stir to create an even layer, submerging all of the pasta.

5. Seal the Foodi and cook on High pressure for 3 minutes with quick release pressure. Remove the lid and add the milk to the pasta.

6. Gently stir while gradually adding the shredded cheese. Reserve 2 ounces of cheddar for the top.

7. Once everything is melted and creamy, add the cooked bacon back to the mac and cheese along with the dry spices.

8. Top with the remaining 2 ounces of shredded cheddar and use the Foodi's broil function for 2-3 minutes until the cheese is melted to your liking.

9. Serve immediately and Enjoy!

Breakfast Casserole

Preparation time: 10 minutes

Cooking time: 15 minutes

Overall time: 25 minutes

Serves: 6 to 8 people

Recipe Ingredients:

- 1 pound of ground sausage
- ¼ cup of diced white onion
- 1 diced green bell pepper
- 8 whole eggs, beaten
- ½ cup of shredded Colby jack cheese
- 1 teaspoon of fennel seed
- ½ teaspoon of garlic salt

Cooking Instructions:

1. Use the sauté function to brown the sausage in the pot of the foodi.

2. Add in the onion and pepper and cook along with the ground sausage until the veggies are soft and the sausage is cooked.

3. Using the 8.75-inch pan or the Air Fryer pan, spray it with non-stick cooking spray. Place the ground sausage mixture on the bottom of the pan.

4. Top evenly with cheese. Pour the beaten eggs evenly over the cheese and sausage. Add fennel seed and garlic salt evenly over the eggs.

5. Place the rack in the low position in the Ninja Foodi, and then place the pan on top. Set to Air Crisp for about 15 minutes at 390°F.

6. Carefully remove and serve.

Sous Vide Egg Bites Quiche

Preparation time: 10 minutes

Cooking time: 15 minutes

Overall time: 25 minutes

Serves: 4 to 6 people

Recipe Ingredients:

- 6 eggs
- 1 cup of cottage cheese
- 1 ½ cup of shredded Gruyere Havarti or Monterey Jack cheese
- ½ cup of shredded Parmesan cheese
- 1 cup of bacon fried and crumbled
- Salt and Pepper

Cooking Instructions:

1. Place ½ cup of the bacon crumbles in the Ninja Foodi round cake pan.

2. Pour 1 cup of water into the Ninja Foodi pressure cooker pan and place the rack over the water.

3. Place the bacon pan on the rack and preheat the Foodi for about 5 minutes and crisp.

4. Crack eggs into a blender and add cottage cheese and 1 cup of shredded gruyere cheese and the parmesan cheese to the blender.

5. Season with salt and pepper, pulse blender till mixture is liquefied. Pour the egg mixture over the crisped up bacon in the cake pan.

6. Place the pressure cooker lid on the Foodi. Set to pressure cook for about 10 minutes. When done cooking release the vent for quick release.

7. Sprinkle the top of the quiche with the remaining shredded cheese and bacon. Put the air crisper lid back down on the Foodi.

8. Set air crisp mode for about four minutes, remove and cut into six slices. Serve immediately and Enjoy!

Breakfast Pizza

Preparation time: 10 minutes

Cooking time: 20 minutes

Overall time: 30 minutes

Serves: 2 to 4 people

Recipe Ingredients:

For the Biscuit Pizza Dough:

- 1 cup (120g) of all-purpose flour
- 1 tablespoon (12g) of granulated sugar
- 1 teaspoon of baking powder
- ¼ teaspoon of kosher salt
- 2/3 cup (150g) of fat free Greek yogurt

For the Toppings:

- 4 slices of center cut bacon, cut into thin strips
- 4 large eggs, beaten
- 2 ounces of reduced fat cream cheese, softened or room temp
- 2 ounces of freshly shredded cheese

Cooking Instructions:

1. Mix the flour, sugar, baking powder, and salt in a large bowl before adding the Greek yogurt. Use a fork to mix everything together until crumbly.

2. Empty the beginnings of the dough onto a flat surface and use your hands to form a ball of dough.

3. Use your knuckles to press outward from the center of the dough, creating thicker edges for the crust than in the center. The dough should be about 8" in diameter.

4. Use a rolling pin here, spray the air fryer basket with cooking spray before adding the crust.

5. Brush the top with a splash of skim milk, egg whites, butter, or a bit more cooking spray. Air crisp at 375°F for about 10 minutes.

6. Flip and air crisp for an additional 3 minutes at 375°F before adding the toppings. While the crust cooks, add the bacon strips to a nonstick skillet over high heat.

7. Once fully cooked, remove the skillet from the heat and add the eggs. Stir to scramble and add the cream cheese once the eggs are nearly cooked and set it aside.

8. Add the bacon and eggs mixture to the crust. Top with the shredded cheese and air fry for an additional 3 to 5 minutes until the cheese is melted and bubbly.

9. Let the pizza cool for a minute or two before carefully transferring out of the air fryer basket and slicing. Enjoy!

Mini Egg Muffins

Preparation time: 5 minutes

Cooking time: 15 minutes

Overall time: 20 minutes

Serves: 2 to 4 people

Recipe Ingredients:

- 2 fully cooked sausage links
- 2 egg yolks
- 1 egg
- Splash of milk
- 3 tablespoons of chopped onion
- Shredded cheese

Cooking Instructions:

1. Whisk together eggs and milk and season to taste. Spray 6 cup muffin pan with non-stick spray.

2. Pour 2 cups of water in bottom of Ninja pan and place muffin pan on top of rack and insert into your Ninja foodi.

3. Sprinkle sausage, onion into each cup. Pour egg mixture into each to fill. Top with shredded cheese.

4. Put paper towel between pot and lid to collect the moisture. Steam bake at 350°F for about 15 minutes.

5. Serve immediately and Enjoy!

Breakfast Frittata

Preparation time: 15 minutes

Cooking time: 30 minutes

Overall time: 45 minutes

Serves: 6 to 8 people

Recipe Ingredients:

- 3 tbsp. of extra virgin olive oil
- 2 medium leeks, white and pale green parts only, thinly sliced, rinsed thoroughly
- 1 package (8 oz.) of cremini mushrooms, thinly sliced
- 12 large eggs
- ½ cup of crème fraiche
- 2 tbsp. of fresh parsley, minced
- 1 cup of shredded Swiss-Gruyère cheese, divided
- ¼ tsp. of kosher salt
- ¼ tsp. of freshly ground black pepper
- 1 cup of water

Cooking Instructions:

1. Select Sauté and set to Medium High, Select Start/Stop button to begin. Add oil and allow to preheat for about 5 minutes.

2. When the 5 minutes is complete, add leeks and cook until softened, about 5 minutes.

3. Then add mushrooms. Cook, stirring often, until liquid has evaporated. While mushrooms are cooking.

4. Whisk together the eggs, crème fraiche, and parsley in a large bowl. Stir in ¾ cup of cheese, salt, and pepper.

5. Once liquid has evaporated, remove mushrooms and leeks from the pot and stir into the egg mixture.

6. Add water to the pot. Place the Ninja multi-purpose pan (or 8-inch baking pan) on the reversible rack, making sure rack is in the lower position.

7. Place rack with pan in pot. Close the crisping lid. Preheat the unit by selecting Boil and setting time to 5 minutes.

8. Select Start/Stop button to begin. When unit is preheated, open the crisping lid and generously spray the pan with cooking spray. Pour egg mixture into the pan.

9. Assemble the pressure lid, making sure the pressure release valve is in the SEAL position. Select Pressure and set to High, set time to 10 minutes.

10. Select Start/Stop button to begin. When pressure cooking is complete, allow the pressure to release naturally for about 10 minutes.

11. After 10 minutes, quick release the remaining pressure by moving the pressure release valve to the Vent position.

12. Carefully remove lid when unit has finished releasing pressure. Pat the surface of the frittata with a paper towel to remove excess moisture.

13. Sprinkle another ¼ cup cheese on top. Close the crisping lid, select Broil, and set time to 7 minutes.

14. Select Start/Stop to begin. When cooking is complete, frittata is ready to serve.

Quiche Lorraine

Preparation time: 10 minutes

Cooking time: 35 minutes

Overall time: 45 minutes

Serves: 4 to 6 people

Recipe Ingredients:

- 8 eggs
- ¼ cup of heavy cream
- 2 tsp. of kosher salt
- Butter, for greasing
- 1 refrigerated store-bought pie crust
- 5 slices of uncooked bacon, cut in 1/4-inch strips
- 1 small onion, peeled, diced
- 1 bag (6 oz.) of fresh spinach
- 1 bunch of fresh chives, finely chopped
- ¼ pound of grated Swiss cheese

Cooking Instructions:

1. In a large bowl, beat the eggs, heavy cream, and salt until smooth. Grease the Ninja multi-purpose pan (or an 8-inch round baking pan) with butter.

2. Place pie crust in pan, covering bottom of pan and pushing into sides. Set pan aside. Select Sauté and set to HIGH. Allow the pan to preheat for about 3 minutes.

3. After the 3 minutes, add bacon to the pot and cook, stirring occasionally, for about 3 minutes. Add onion and cook until translucent, about 3 minutes.

4. Add spinach and cook until wilted, about 2 minutes. Carefully remove pot from unit and place on a heat-resistant surface.

5. Stir in egg mixture, along with the chives and cheese. Transfer mixture to a bowl and set it aside.

6. Place pot back into unit and place pan with pie dough on reversible rack, making sure the rack is in the lower orientation.

7. Place rack with pan in pot and close the crisping lid. Select Bake/Roast, set temperature to 400°F, and set time to 8 minutes.

8. Select Stat/Stop to begin. Pour egg mixture into browned crust. Close the crisping lid; select Bake/Roast, set temperature to 360°F, and set time to 17 minutes.

9. Select START/STOP to begin. When cooking is complete, carefully remove pan from pot.

10. Allow quiche to cool fully in the refrigerator before removing from multi-purpose pan and serving.

LUNCH RECIPES

Pot Roast

Preparation time: 10 minutes

Cooking time: 1 hour

Overall time 1 hour 10 minutes

Serves: 4 to 6 people

Recipe Ingredients:

- 2 tablespoons of vegetable oil
- 3 pounds of chuck roast
- 1 teaspoon of salt
- 1.5 cups of beef broth
- 5 teaspoons of sage
- 5 teaspoons of black pepper
- 1 teaspoon of crushed red pepper
- 1 pound of baby carrots
- 1 pound of mushrooms

Cooking Instructions:

1. Select Sear/Saute on your Ninja Foodi. Press Start and allow pot to preheat.

2. It takes about 3 to 5 minutes. Add vegetable oil to pot. Cook for about 2 minutes. Sprinkle salt on both sides of the beef roast. Pat dry, add beef to preheated pot.

3. Heat the beef for 3-5 minutes on each side (until brown). Transfer beef to wire rack. If there is any oil left in the pot, empty it.

4. Add beef broth, sage, and peppers. Bring to a boil. Add the beef back to the pot. Close Pressure lid, adjust pressure to High and cook time 60 minutes.

5. Press Start and use quick pressure release. Add carrots and mushrooms. Close lid and cook on High pressure for about 2 minutes.

6. Use quick release. Serve immediately and Enjoy!

Steak and Vegetable Bowls

Preparation time: 5 minutes

Cooking time: 15 minutes

Overall time: 20 minutes

Serves: 4 to 6 people

Recipe Ingredients:

- 2 kc strip of steaks
- 1 cup of red bell pepper, diced
- 1 cup of green bell pepper, diced
- 1 cup of yellow squash, diced
- 1 cup of mushroom, sliced
- ¼ cup of white onion, diced
- ½ tablespoon of steak seasoning
- Olive oil cooking spray

Cooking Instructions:

1. Cut the steak into smaller cubed chunks. Spray the basket of the air fryer or ninja foodi basket.

2. Place the steaks and vegetables in the air fryer or ninja foodi basket. Sprinkle evenly with the seasoning. Spray with olive oil spray.

3. Cook for about 7 minutes on 390°F and carefully open the lid when the time is up, stir and mix the ingredients, coat with additional olive oil spray.

4. Cook for an additional 8 minutes at 390°F or until done to your preference. Serve immediately and Enjoy!

Mostaccioli

Preparation time: 5 minutes

Cooking time: 15 minutes

Overall time: 20 minutes

Serves: 4 to 6 people

Recipe Ingredients:

- 1 tsp. of olive oil
- ½ cup of diced onions
- 1 lb. of lean ground beef
- ½ lb. of ground beef
- Ground chicken or Italian sausage
- 1 tbsp. of garlic- minced
- 1 tsp. of sugar
- 1 tbsp. of Italian seasoning
- ½ tsp. of red pepper flakes
- Red pepper flakes
- 2 cans of beef broth
- 1 cup of water
- 1 (24 oz.) jar of pasta sauce
- 1 lb. of dried mostaccioli noodles
- 2 cups of mozzarella cheese

Cooking Instructions:

1. Turn your Ninja Foodi on to Saute High mode and add Olive Oil Add onions, ground beef and garlic.

2. Continue to sauté until beef is evenly browned. Turn off the Ninja Foodi. Add sugar, Italian seasoning and red pepper flakes.

3. Pour in pasta sauce and pour 1 cup of water into pasta sauce jar- shake- pour water mixture into Ninja Foodi pot.

4. Pour 2 cans of beef broth into Ninja Foodi pot and stir beef and liquid until well combined.

5. Pour in mostaccioli pasta Don't stir, make sure that all pasta is covered by liquid. Pushed down on the noodles with a spatula until they were covered with liquid.

6. Close the pressure cooker lid, turn Ninja Foodi back on and cook on high for about 3 minutes.

7. Once the timer goes off, natural release pressure for 3 minutes. Quick release remaining pressure.

8. Turn off Ninja Foodi. Open the pressure cooker lid and stir pasta together. Be sure to stir well and ensure no pasta is clumped together.

9. Add in 1 cup of shredded mozzarella cheese and stir. Sprinkle remaining 1 cup of mozzarella cheese on top.

10. Using the broiler lid, close lid and broil on high for about 5 minutes or just until cheese is melted and golden brown.

11. Serve immediately and Enjoy!

Pulled Pork

Preparation time: 5 minutes

Cooking time: 10 minutes

Overall time: 15 minutes

Serves: 2 to 4 people

Recipe Ingredients:

- 20 oz. of young green jackfruit
- ½ teaspoon of liquid smoke
- 1 cup of water or vegetable broth
- 1 cup of barbeque of sauce
- 1 teaspoon of garlic powder
- ½ teaspoon of onion powder
- 1 teaspoon of paprika
- 1 ½ teaspoons of seasoning salt
- Pepper, to taste

Cooking Instructions:

1. Open and drain the young green jackfruit from the can. With two forks, pull the jackfruit apart, to resemble pulled pork.

2. Place the jackfruit in the Foodi bowl, and season with the seasoning salt, pepper, garlic, onion and paprika.

3. Add the 1 cup of water or vegetable stock Place the pressure-cooking lid on the top, place the toggle switch on seal.

4. Manually pressure cook on high mode for about 5 minutes. Broil for about 10 minutes at 400°F until the ends of the jackfruit begin to caramelize. Enjoy!

Pot Roast

Preparation time: 15 minutes

Cooking time: 1 hour 30 minutes

Overall time: 1 hour 45 minutes

Serves: 6 to 8 people

Recipe Ingredients:

- 3.5 pounds of beef bottom round roast
- 2 tablespoons of homemade ranch seasoning mix
- ½ cup of warm water
- 2 teaspoons of beef bouillon
- 8 tablespoons of butter
- 7 Greek pepperoncini peppers

Cooking Instructions:

1. Add the roast to the Ninja Foodi pot. Warm your water in the microwave for 1 minute.

2. Stir in the beef bouillon and sprinkle the roast with the spice mixture and pour on the bouillon broth.

3. Top with a stick of butter and the peppers. Sit the cooking pot in the Foodi base and twist & lock the pressure cooker lid.

4. Double check that your vent on the lid is turned to "seal" Plug in your Ninja Foodi, select Pressure Cooker, and cook on High mode for about 1 hours 30 minutes.

5. Once the clock reaches zero, you can allow the pressure to release normally. You can release the pressure quickly by turning your vent on the lid from seal to vent.

6. Serve immediately and Enjoy!

One-Pot Pasta Primavera

Preparation time: 5 minutes

Cooking time: 20 minutes

Overall time: 23 minutes

Serves: 2 to 4 people

Recipe Ingredients:

- 2 cups of water
- 1/2 tablespoon of vegetable base
- 8 oz. of linguine
- 1 red onion chopped in large chunks
- 1 cup of green beans cut in half
- 1 cup of cherry tomatoes cut in half
- 1 cup of orange Pepper 1 1/2" chunks
- ½ teaspoon of sea salt
- 1 bulb of roasted garlic
- 1 cup of spinach see post for various vegetable choices
- ½ cup of peas
- 3 oz. of parmesan cheese about 1 cup grated
- 4 tablespoons of butter (salted) optional, but delicious
- Freshly cracked black pepper or red pepper flakes

Cooking Instructions:

1. Chop the pepper and onions into 1 ½" chunks, slice the cherry tomatoes in ½ and cut the green beans in half.

2. Place 2 cups of water in the inner pot, add vegetable base. Place the onion chunks in the bottom of the inner pot.

3. It will create a little barrier so the pasta noodles don't stick to the bottom. Break the linguine noodles in half.

4. Layer them a handful at a time in a criss cross method. Add the salt and the cut up vegetables on top, except for the spinach and peas.

5. When the pressure cooking is complete, add them. Put the pressure lid on and make sure the vent is to seal.

6. Set the Ninja Foodi on high pressure for about 3 minutes. When the time is up, allow the Ninja Foodi to natural release for about 2 minutes.

7. Manually release the remaining pressure add the fresh spinach and peas and stir the noodles and the vegetables around so the spinach and peas are incorporated into the pasta.

8. Close the Tender Crisp lid and let it rest for about 5 minutes to give the spinach time to wilt a bit.

9. Place 1 tablespoon of salted butter in the bottom of a bowl and place the pasta primavera o

10. n top. Add grated Parmesan Cheese and fresh cracked black pepper or red pepper flakes. Serve & Enjoy!

Greek Chicken and Veggies

Preparation time: 10 minutes

Cooking time: 30 minutes

Overall time: 40 minutes

Serves: 3 to 5 people

Recipe Ingredients:

For the Veggies:

- 1 medium (200g) red onion, diced (large)
- 1 large (250g) bell pepper, diced (large)
- 1 pint of grape tomatoes
- 1 tablespoon of olive oil
- 1 teaspoon of black pepper
- 1 teaspoon of garlic powder
- 1 teaspoon of onion powder
- ½ teaspoon of dried oregano

For the Greek chicken:

- 1 pound of boneless skinless chicken breast, diced
- 1 tablespoon of olive oil
- 1 tablespoon of Greek seasoning
- 1 teaspoon of black pepper

Cooking Instructions:

1. Cut the onion and bell pepper into 1" pieces and place in a large bowl with the tomatoes.

2. Toss the veggies with the 1 tablespoon of of olive oil and spices before placing in the air fryer basket.

3. Cook for about 10 minutes at 400°F. In the same bowl, add the diced chicken, remaining olive oil, Greek seasoning, and black pepper.

4. Stir to fully coat the chicken. After the veggies have cooked for 10 minutes, transfer to a clean bowl and set it aside.

5. Add the chicken to the air fryer basket and cook for about 8 minutes at 400°F. After the chicken is cooked, add the veggies back to the basket.

6. Use the Foodi's broil function for about 6 to 8 minutes or until the onion/peppers begin to slightly char and the tomatoes begin to wrinkle.

7. Serve with kalamata olives, crumbled feta cheese, parsley, rice, and lemon juice, if desired.

Quick & Easy Ninja Foodi Spaghetti

Preparation time: 5 minutes

Cooking time: 20 minutes

Overall time: 25 minutes

Serves: 4 to 6 people

Recipe Ingredients:

- 1 lb. of ground Italian sausage
- 3 garlic cloves, chopped
- 1 small onion, chopped
- 1 tsp. of salt
- 2 tsp. of Italian Seasoning of choice
- 1 tsp. of olive oil
- ½ cup of chicken broth
- 3 cups of water
- 1 cup of fresh grape tomatoes
- 18.3 ounces of jar crushed tomatoes
- 1 lb. of spaghetti noodles
- Fresh basil as garnish (optional)
- Fresh shredded parmesan cheese as garnish (optional)

Cooking Instructions:

1. Use the sear/sauté function on the Ninja Foodi to sauté the garlic and onions with the olive oil.

2. Add the ground sausage and brown the meat until cooked through and break up the sausage into desired size.

3. Once meat is cooked, turn off the sear function and add the broth. Stir and scrape up any pieces of meat off of the bottom of the cook pan.

4. Add the grape tomatoes and crushed tomatoes. There is no need to stir the ingredients.

5. Gently add the water to the pan and break up the spaghetti noodles in half and loosely layer in criss cross pattern.

6. Loosely layer the pasta to avoid it clumping together and to properly cook during pressure cooking. Add the pressure-cooking lid and set the vent to the seal position.

7. Set the pressure cook time to zero and press start. The time to come to pressure will be about 10 minutes or so.

8. Once the pressure has been reached, set a timer for about 10 minutes and allow for natural pressure release.

9. After the 10 minutes of natural pressure release, switch the vent to release any remaining pressure. Then carefully remove the lid.

10. Gently stir the pasta. Allow for a few minutes of rest time for any extra liquid to absorb. Serve with basil and freshly shredded parmigiano cheese if desired.

Hamburger Stroganoff

Preparation time: 5 minutes

Cooking time: 15 minutes

Overall time: 20 minutes

Serves: 2 to 4 people

Recipe Ingredients:

- 1 medium yellow onion, diced
- 1 clove of garlic, minced
- 1 pound of 80/20 hamburger
- 1 teaspoon of salt
- ¼ teaspoon of pepper
- 10,5-ounces cream of mushroom soup
- 1 tablespoon of flour
- 3 cups of beef broth
- 1 package of egg noodles
- 1 cup of sour cream

Cooking Instructions:

1. First, spray the inside of your Ninja Foodi with nonstick cooking spray. This will help keep the hamburger from sticking to the pot.

2. Turn the Ninja Foodi to saute and let it heat up for a few minutes. Then add the hamburger, onion, and garlic to the Ninja Foodi.

3. While you are browning the hamburger break it up into bite-size pieces. Once the beef is browned, sprinkle the flour over the meat/onion/garlic mixture.

4. Pour in the beef broth, cream of mushroom soup, salt, and pepper. Be sure to stir it well until it's all combined.

5. Add the egg noodles. Place the pressure-cooking lid on the Ninja Foodi and lock it shut.

6. Make sure the vent is closed. Set the Ninja Foodi on pressure cook high for about 8 minutes.

7. When the timer goes off, let the pressure naturally release for about 5 minutes, let the Ninja Foodi switch to the warm mode.

8. Do a quick release to let the remaining pressure out, once the pressure has been released you will be able to unlock the lid and remove it.

9. Then, stir in the sour cream until it's rich and creamy. Now it's time to serve it and enjoy!

Rigatoni

Preparation time: 5 minutes

Cooking time: 15 minutes

Overall time: 20 minutes

Serves: 2 to 4 people

Recipe Ingredients:

- 1 pound of ground turkey
- 1 pound of rigatoni
- 2 jars of pasta sauce
- Chicken/beef broth
- Minced garlic
- Onion powder

Cooking Instructions:

1. Brown the meat with onion powder and garlic on sear/sauté and drain if needed.

2. Pour sauce over meat, add broth of your choice to half of each jar and shake to get all the sauce, stir a little.

3. Put pasta over sauce but do not stir. Add enough water to just cover pasta. Pressure Cook for about 5 minutes.

4. Do a natural pressure release for about 5 minutes, after that allow pressure to be released manually.

5. Top with cheese and broil until cheese is browned for about 4 to 5 minutes. You can add ricotta to make it creamy.

DINNER RECIPES

Shrimp Boil Recipe

Preparation time: 10 minutes

Cooking time: 15 minutes

Overall time 25 minutes

Serves: 4 to 6 people

Recipe Ingredients:

- 1 pound of red potatoes cut in half
- 4 ears of fresh corn snapped in half
- 12 ounces of Cajun style andouille sausage cut into 2 inch pieces
- 4 cups of water
- 1 ½ tablespoons of Zataran's shrimp boil liquid
- 3 teaspoons of old bay seasoning divided
- 1 pound of fresh shrimp peeled and deveined
- 1 pound of fresh mussels
- Fresh chopped parsley optional
- Lemon slices optional

Garlic Butter for Dipping:

- ½ cup of butter melted
- ½ teaspoon of garlic powder

Cooking Instructions:

1. Add red potatoes, corn, sausage, water, shrimp boil liquid, and 2 teaspoons old bay to the Ninja Foodi insert and stir.

2. Cover and cook on high pressure for about 4 minutes. Once timer is complete, do a quick release and open lid once all pressure is released.

3. Add shrimp and mussels and 1 teaspoon of old bay and stir. Cover and cook on high pressure for 1 minute.

4. Once timer goes off, allow to natural release for about 2 minutes, then quick release remaining pressure.

5. Combine butter and garlic powder in a separate bowl and use as a dipping sauce. Sprinkle with parsley and serve with lemon on the side. Enjoy

Salsa Chicken Tacos

Preparation time: 5 minutes

Cooking time: 15 minutes

Overall time: 20 minutes

Serves: 2 to 4 people

Recipe Ingredients:

- 1.5 pounds of chicken breast, boneless and skinless
- 2 teaspoons of ancho chili powder
- 1 teaspoon of ground cumin
- ½ teaspoon of ground coriander
- ¼ teaspoon of salt
- ¼ teaspoon of ground pepper
- 1 clove garlic, minced
- 1 cup of fire roasted salsa
- 2 tablespoons of cilantro, fresh chopped
- Taco fixings
- Tortillas

Cooking Instructions:

1. Plug the Ninja Foodi in and make sure you have the pressure cooking lid. In a small bowl combine the ancho chili powder, cumin, coriander, salt, and pepper.

2. Make sure to stir it together to ensure it is mixed very well. Coat each side of your chicken in the spice mixture you just made.

3. Place the chicken in the Ninja Foodi and sprinkle the garlic over the chicken. Pour the fire roasted salsa over the chicken. Be sure to cover the chicken with the salsa.

4. Place the pressure lid on the Ninja Foodi with the vent closed. Set it to pressure, high, for about 13 minutes.

5. When your Ninja Foodi beeps, do a quick release. Once the pressure is released, open the Ninja Foodi and remove the chicken.

6. Shred the chicken. (You can use two forks to shred my chicken). Then return the chicken to the Ninja Foodi.

7. Add the cilantro and stir. Now you are ready to serve! Take a tortilla and scoop some chicken onto it, add your favorite toppings and enjoy!

Corned Beef and Cabbage

Preparation time: 10 minutes

Cooking time: 1 hour 25 minutes

Overall time: 1 hour 35 minutes

Serves: 6 to 8 people

Recipe Ingredients:

- 4 to 5 lb. corned beef brisket
- 1 cup of chicken stock
- ¼ cup of balsamic vinegar
- 1 onion, diced
- 7 cloves of garlic, peeled
- ½ teaspoon of dried thyme leaves
- 3 bay leaves
- 1 ½ lb. of gold baby potatoes, scrubbed
- 1 lb. of carrots, peeled and cut into large pieces
- 1 head green cabbage, cored and cut in wedges

For glaze:

- ½ cup of light brown sugar, packed
- ½ cup of water
- 1/2 cup of Dijon mustard

Cooking Instructions:

1. Place brisket in the cooker pot with the fat-side down. Add seasoning packet, stock, balsamic vinegar, onion, garlic, thyme, and bay leaves.

2. Cover the cooker with lid and set the valve to sealing, set the Ninja foodi to pressure cook for about 75 minutes.

3. Press start/stop button to begin the cooking cycle. Once the cycle is complete, allow the pressure to naturally release for about 10 minutes before quick release.

4. Remove the brisket from the cooker and keep warm. Also remove the garlic and bay leaves. Add the potatoes, carrots, and cabbage to the pot with the liquid.

5. Cover the cooker with lid and set the valve to sealing. Set the Ninja foodi to pressure cook for about 3 minutes.

6. Use the start/stop to begin the cooking cycle. Once the cycle is complete, quick release the pressure.

7. In a small saucepan, heat the brown sugar and water over medium-high heat until it comes to a boil.

8. Stir in the mustard and continue cooking until the sauce is reduced, for about 2 to 3 minutes.

9. Place the corned beef brisket over the vegetables and pour the glaze over the corned beef. Replace the crisping lid and set the Air Crisp function to 400°F.

10. Cook for about 20 minutes. Remove brisket and allow it to rest for about 15 minutes prior to slicing.

11. Slice brisket against the grain. Serve with vegetables and mustard, if desired.

Cheesy Beef and Potatoes

Preparation time: 5 minutes

Cooking time: 27 minutes

Overall time: 32 minutes

Serves: 3 to 5 people

Recipe Ingredients:

- 2 ½ lb. of ground beef
- 6 to 8 russet potatoes, peeled and sliced (1/4" thick)
- 1 tsp. of onion powder
- 1 tsp. of garlic powder
- ¾ cup of heavy cream
- 1 cup of chicken broth
- 3 cups of sharp cheddar cheese, grated

Cooking Instructions:

1. Close the crisping lid and press the Air Crisp button, set temperature to 390°F. Air Crisp for about 10 minutes.

2. It will give it a nice crispy brownish color. Open lid, give it a good stir. Close the lid and Air Crisp for another 5 minutes.

3. Open lid and pour 1 cup of cheese over the top, smooth to cover the top completely. Air Crisp for a few minutes until cheese is melted and bubbly.

4. Dinner is served!

Fall Apart Ham

Preparation time: 10 minutes

Cooking time: 50 minutes

Overall time: 1 hour

Serves: 2 to 4 people

Recipe Ingredients:

- 8 lb. of bone-in ham
- 1 cup of Coca-Cola
- 1 cup of apple juice
- 20 oz. can of pineapple slices, divided

Cooking Instructions:

1. In your Ninja Foodi cooking pot, combine Coca-Cola, apple juice and ¾ of the container of pineapple slices.

2. Place ham in the cooking pot, flat side down. Place remaining pineapple slices on top. Select High Pressure for about 50 minutes.

3. Allow to be released naturally for about 10 minutes, then do a quick pressure release.

4. Baste ham with juice in Foodi, slice and serve.

Creamy Chicken

Preparation time: 5 minutes

Cooking time: 8 minutes

Overall time: 30 minutes

Serves: 4 to 6 people

Recipe Ingredients:

- 4 large boneless chicken breasts
- 1 cup of chicken broth
- 1.5 tsp. of minced garlic
- 1.5 tsp. of Italian seasoning
- ¼ tsp. of salt
- ¼ tsp. of pepper
- ½ cup of heavy cream
- 1/2 cup of roasted red peppers- diced
- 1.5 tbsp. of corn starch
- 2 tbsp. water
- 1.5 tbsp. of basil pesto

For chicken sauce:

- 4 large boneless chicken breasts
- 1 3/4 cups of chicken broth
- 3 tsp. of minced garlic
- 3 tsp. of Italian seasoning
- ½ tsp. of salt
- ½ tsp. of pepper
- 1 cup of heavy cream
- 1 cup of roasted red peppers- diced
- 3 tbsp. of corn starch
- 4 tbsp. of water
- 3 tbsp. of basil pesto

Cooking Instructions:

1. Place the chicken breasts into the Ninja Foodi pot. Pour in 1 cup of chicken broth.

2. Sprinkle 1.5 teaspoons of Italian seasoning on to the chicken. Spread 1.5 teaspoons of minced garlic on to chicken.

3. Add ¼ teaspoon of salt and a ¼ teaspoon of pepper. Close the pressure cooker lid. Move valve to "seal" position.

4. Choose the pressure mode set time to 7 minutes. When timer beeps, naturally release pressure for about 5 minutes.

5. After 5 minutes, quick release remaining pressure and carefully open lid. Remove chicken from pot using tongs and set chicken aside.

6. Turn Ninja Foodi on to the sauté function and high mode for about 15 minutes. Pour in 1/2 cup diced red peppers and stir.

7. Pour in ½ cup of heavy cream. Add in 1.5 tablespoons of pesto. Make corn starch slurry by combining 1.5 tablespoons of corn starch with 2 tablespoons of water.

8. Pour in corn starch slurry and stir. Allow sauce to sauté for about 5 minutes. Be sure to stir regularly.

9. Once sauce has achieved desired thickness, add chicken back in or serve by pouring gravy over chicken.

10. Serve with your favorite side dishes.

Hawaiian Barbeque Chicken and Rice

Preparation time: 15 minutes

Cooking time: 25 minutes

Overall time: 40 minutes

Serves: 3 to 5 people

Recipe Ingredients:

- 2 tablespoons of olive oil, divided
- ¼ cup of white onion chopped
- 1 pound of chicken cubed
- ½ cup of fresh pineapple diced
- ½ cup of zucchini
- 1 teaspoon of salt
- ¼ teaspoon of pepper
- 1 whole jalapeno sliced
- 3/8 cup barbeque sauce, gluten free
- 1 cup of white rice
- 1 cup of water

Cooking Instructions:

1. Set Ninja Foodi or Instant Pot to sauté on Medium/High, add 1 tablespoon of olive oil and onions.

2. Sauté the onions until they're translucent. Add another 1 tablespoon of olive oil, chicken, salt, and pepper.

3. Stir constantly until chicken is browned or cooked through. Once chicken is browned, add zucchini, pineapple, jalapenos and Barbeque sauce.

4. Stir Until all ingredients are coated. Add water and rice. Add pressure cooker lid. Set to cook on high mode for about 3 minutes.

5. When pressure cooking is finished, release pressure quickly and serve immediately!

Homemade Pot Pie

Preparation time: 10 minutes

Cooking time: 35 minutes

Overall time: 45 minutes

Serves: 4 to 6 people

Recipe Ingredients:

- 4 tablespoons (½ stick) of unsalted butter
- 1 onion, diced
- 2 garlic cloves, minced
- 2 pounds of boneless chicken or turkey breasts, cut into 1-inch cubes
- 2 Yukon Gold potatoes, diced
- 1 cup of chicken broth
- ½ teaspoon of sea salt
- ½ teaspoon of freshly ground black pepper
- 1 (16 oz.) bag mixed frozen vegetables
- ½ cup of heavy (whipping) cream
- 1 store-bought refrigerated raw piecrust, at room temperature

Cooking Instructions:

1. Select Sear/Sauté and set it to Medium-High. Select Start/Stop to begin. Allow the pot to preheat for about 5 minutes.

2. Put the butter, onion, and garlic in the preheated pot and sauté until the onion softened, for about 3 minutes.

3. Add the chicken or turkey, potatoes, and broth to the pot. Season with the salt and black pepper.

4. Assemble the Pressure Lid, making sure the pressure release valve is in the Seal position.

5. Select Pressure and set to High. Set the time to 10 minutes, then select Start/Stop to begin.

6. When pressure cooking is complete, quick release the pressure by moving the pressure release valve to the vent position.

7. Carefully remove the lid when the pressure has finished releasing. Select Sear/Sauté and set it to Medium-High.

8. Select Start/Stop to begin, add the frozen vegetables and cream to the pot. Stir until the sauce thickens and bubbles, for about 3 minutes.

9. Lay the piecrust evenly on top of the filling mixture, folding over the edges if necessary.

10. Make a small cut in the center of the crust so that steam can escape during baking. Close the Crisping Lid.

11. Select Broil and set the time to 10 minutes. Select Start/Stop to begin. When cooking is complete, remove the pot from the Ninja Food.

12. Place it on a heat-resistant surface. Let the potpie rest for about 10 to 15 minutes before serving.

Buttery Ranch Pork Chops

Preparation time: 10 minutes

Cooking time: 20 minutes

Overall time: 30 minutes

Serves: 4 to 6 people

Recipe Ingredients:

- 8 pork chops
- 1/3 cup of butter
- 1 cup of chicken broth
- 1 packet of Hidden Valley Ranch Dressing
- salt and pepper, to taste
- 1 tablespoon of cornstarch
- 2 tablespoons of water
- ¼ cup of sour cream (optional)

Cooking Instructions:

1. Wash and pat dry the pork chops. Season with salt and pepper Turn the Foodi onto sauté and add 1 tablespoon of butter to melt.

2. Sauté the chops for about 3 to 4 minutes per side until they have a nice golden caramelization on each side. Add the chicken broth in the bottom of the bowl.

3. Sprinkle the ranch seasoning over the chops Dot the butter in various places over and around the chops.

4. Select the Manual pressure function and set on high mode for 10 minutes. Be sure to turn the toggle on the pressure lid to sealing.

5. When time is complete, Do a natural release for 15 minutes. QR the rest of the pressure after time is up. Carefully remove the lid after the silver pin drops.

6. Remove the chops and tent with foil to keep warm. Make the slurry of cornstarch and water, and pour it into the Foodi bowl.

7. Switch the machine onto Sauté mode. Add the sour cream now, stir until the sauce thickens.

8. Place chops back into the sauce for a minute or two and then serve them over rice or potatoes, etc. Enjoy!

Meatloaf and Potatoes

Preparation time: 15 minutes

Cooking time: 35 minutes

Overall time: 50 minutes

Serves: 4 to 6 people

Recipe Ingredients:

Meatloaf:

- 2 lb. of ground beef
- 2 eggs, beaten
- 2 cups of old-fashioned oats or gluten-free old-fashioned oats
- ½ cup of evaporated milk
- ½ cup of chopped onion
- ½ teaspoon of garlic salt

Potatoes:

- 3 lb. of peeled potatoes, russet or yellow
- 1 cup of water
- 1 cup of cream (1/2 and 1/2)
- ¼ cup of sour cream
- 4 tablespoons of unsalted butter
- 1 teaspoon of garlic salt or to taste

Corn:

- 12 ounces of frozen corn
- 1 tablespoon of unsalted butter

Sauce:

- 1 cup of ketchup
- ¾ cup of brown sugar, packed
- ¼ cup of chopped onion
- ½ teaspoon of liquid smoke
- ¼ teaspoon of garlic powder

Cooking Instructions:

1. In a large bowl, combine all ingredients for the meatloaf. Spray a sheet of foil with non-stick cooking spray, shape the meatloaf and place on the foil and set it aside.

2. Wash your hands, then cut the potatoes into quarters. Place the potatoes in the bottom of the Ninja Foodi with 1 cup of water.

3. Place the rack inside the foodi where it extends up to the top of the pot. Place the meatloaf on the rack. Set to pressure cook on high mode for about 25 minutes.

4. While this is cooking, prepare the sauce by combining all ingredients in a small saucepan on medium heat. Whisk it until the sugar has dissolved and set aside.

5. Quick-release the pressure. Carefully remove the rack with the meatloaf on it and set aside. Carefully remove the pot and pour the potatoes into a large bowl.

6. Add the rack back into the foodi; however, this time place the rack where it's low in the pot. Simply changing the handles on the side, flip them the other way.

7. Pour the corn onto a sheet of foil with the sides up. Add the butter on top of the corn. Place the meatloaf and corn on the rack in the foodi.

8. Coat the meatloaf with the sauce. Place the foodi on broil for about 5 minutes at 450°F. Open and stir up the corn. Broil an additional 5 minutes.

9. While this is broiling, mash the potatoes with a hand masher and stir in the remaining ingredients.

10. Add additional salt to taste if needed. Remove the meatloaf and corn. Serve!

POULTRY RECIPES

Hard Boiled Eggs

Preparation time: 5 minutes

Cooking time: 8 minutes

Overall time: 13 minutes

Serves: 6 to 8 people

Recipe Ingredients:

- 8 eggs
- 1 cup of water

Cooking Instructions:

1. Dump in 1 cup of Water into pressure cooker.

2. Add 8 eggs in your Ninja Foodi on your metal rack. Close with pressure cooker lid and seal steam release closed.

3. Cook on high for about 8 minutes for perfect eggs. Release for hard boiled eggs. Quickly release the pressure.

4. Once the pressure is released, remove eggs with tongs and place in cold water or ice water bath.

5. This stops the eggs from continuing cooking and make for easier peeling. Put eggs in an ice bath for about 15 minutes.

6. Peel and serve.

Egg and Avocado

Preparation time: 5 minutes

Cooking time: 10 minutes

Overall time: 15 minutes

Serves: 2 to 4 people

Recipe Ingredients:

- 1 Avocado
- Salt and Pepper to taste
- Cooking spray and tin foil
- 2 eggs

Cooking Instructions:

1. Cut avocado in half Scoop some out. Place a cracked egg in each half of the avocado.

2. Add salt and pepper to taste and top with cheese Place on sprayed foil squares and place into air fry basket. Air Crisp at 390°F for about 11 to 12 minutes

3. Plate, serve and Enjoy!

Chicken Pot Pie

Preparation time: 10 minutes

Cooking time: 25 minutes

Overall time: 35 minutes

Serves: 4 to 6 people

Recipe Ingredients:

- ½ stick of unsalted butter
- 1/2 large onion, peeled, diced
- 1 large carrot, peeled, diced
- 2 cloves of garlic, peeled, minced
- 2 lb. of uncooked boneless skinless chicken breasts, cut in 1-inch cubes
- 1 cup of chicken broth
- 1 stalk celery, diced
- ½ cup of frozen peas
- 1 ½ tsp. of fresh thyme, minced
- 1 tbsp. of fresh Italian parsley, minced
- 2 tsp. of kosher salt
- ½ tsp. of black pepper
- ½ cup of heavy cream
- ¼ cup of all-purpose flour
- 1 refrigerated store-bought pie crust, room temperature

Cooking Instructions:

1. Select Sear/Sauté and set to mid: high and select Start/Stop to begin. Allow to preheat for about 5 minutes.

2. After the 5 minutes, add butter to pot. Once it melts, add onion, carrot, and garlic, and Sauté until softened, for about 3 minutes.

3. Add chicken and broth to the pot. Assemble pressure lid, making sure the Pressure Release valve is in the Seal position.

4. Select Pressure and set to High. Set time to 5 minutes. Select Start/Stop button to begin.

5. When pressure cooking is complete, quick release the pressure by moving the Pressure Release valve to the Vent position.

6. Carefully remove lid when unit has finished releasing pressure. Select Sear/Sauté and set to Mid: High.

7. Select Start/Stop to begin. Add remaining ingredients to pot, except pie crust. Stir until sauce thickens and bubbles, about 3 minutes.

8. Lay pie crust evenly on top of the filling mixture, folding over edges if necessary. Make a small cut in center of pie crust so that steam can escape during baking.

9. Close the crisping lid. Select Broil and set time to 10 minutes. Select Start/Stop to begin.

10. When cooking is complete, remove pot from unit and place on a heat-resistant surface. Let it rest for scout 10 to 15 minutes before serving.

Breaded Chicken Tenders & Roasted Broccoli

Preparation time: 15 minutes

Cooking time: 15 minutes

Overall time: 30 minutes

Serves: 2 to 4 people

Recipe Ingredients:

- 1 cup of all-purpose flour
- 2 eggs, beaten
- 1 cup of water, divided
- 2 cups of Italian bread crumbs
- 1 lb. of uncooked chicken tenderloins
- 1 large broccoli crown, cut in 2-inch florets
- 1 tsp. of kosher salt

For Serving:

- Ketchup
- Honey mustard
- Ranch dressing

Cooking Instructions:

1. Place flour in a shallow bowl or plate. Add eggs and 2 tablespoons water to another bowl, whisking to combine. Place bread crumbs into a third bowl or plate.

2. Working in small batches, toss chicken in flour. Tap off excess, then coat chicken in egg wash.

3. Transfer chicken to bread crumbs, tossing well to evenly coat and set it aside. Place broccoli and ½ cup of water in the pot.

4. Assemble pressure lid, making sure the Pressure Release valve is in Sealing position.

5. Select Pressure and set to Low mode, set time to 0 minutes, the time the unit takes to pressurize is long enough to partially cook the broccoli.

6. Select Start/Stop button to begin. When cooking time is complete, quick release the pressure by moving the Pressure Release valve to the Vent position.

7. Carefully remove lid when unit has finished releasing pressure. Place reversible rack in pot over the broccoli, making sure it is in the higher position.

8. Lay chicken tenders on rack, spacing out evenly without overlapping. Close crisping lid.

9. Select the Bake/Roast, set temperature to 360°F, and set time to 12 minutes. Select Start/Stop button to begin.

10. When cooking is complete, season chicken and broccoli with salt and serve with your favorites.

Crispy Chicken Thighs with Carrots & Rice Pilaf

Preparation time: 10 minutes

Cooking time: 15 minutes

Overall time: 25 minutes

Serves: 2 to 4 people

Recipe Ingredients:

- 1 box (6 oz.) of rice pilaf
- 1 ¾ cups of water
- 1 tbsp. of butter
- 4 carrots, peeled, cut in half, lengthwise
- 4 uncooked boneless skin-on chicken thighs
- 2 tbsp. of honey, warmed
- ½ tsp. of smoked paprika
- ½ tsp. of ground cumin
- 2 tsp. of kosher salt, divided
- 1 tbsp. of extra virgin olive oil
- 2 tsp. of poultry spice

Cooking Instructions:

1. Place rice pilaf, water, and butter into pot; stir to incorporate. Place reversible rack in the pot, making sure rack is in the higher position.

2. Place carrots in center of rack. Arrange chicken thighs, skin side up, around the carrots.

3. Assemble pressure lid, making sure the Pressure Release valve is in Sealing position.

4. Select Pressure and set to High mode. Set time to 4 minutes. Select Start/Stop button to begin.

5. While chicken and rice are cooking, stir together warm honey, smoked paprika, cumin, and 1 teaspoon salt and set aside.

6. When pressure cooking is complete, quick release the pressure by moving the Pressure Release valve to the Vent position.

7. Carefully remove lid when unit has finished releasing pressure. Brush carrots with seasoned honey.

8. Brush chicken with olive oil, then season evenly with poultry spice and remaining salt. Close crisping lid. Select BROIL and set time to 10 minutes.

9. Select Start/Stop button to begin. When cooking is complete, serve chicken with carrots and rice.

Chili Rubbed Chicken & Chimichurri

Preparation time: 15 minutes

Cooking time: 35 minutes

Overall time: 50 minutes

Serves: 1 to 3 people

Recipe Ingredients:

- 2 tsp. of kosher salt
- 1 tbsp. of ground paprika
- 1 tbsp. of chili powder
- 1 tbsp. of ground fennel
- 1 tsp. of fresh cracked black pepper
- 1 tsp. of onion powder
- 1 tsp. of garlic powder
- 1 tsp. of ground cumin
- 2 uncooked bone-in, skin-on chicken breasts (3/4–1 1/4 pounds each)
- 1 tbsp. of canola oil

Chimichurri:

- ¼ cup of olive oil
- ½ bunch of fresh cilantro
- ½ bunch of fresh parsley
- 1 shallot, peeled, cut in quarters
- 4 cloves of garlic, peeled
- Zest and juice of 1 lemon
- 1 tsp. of kosher salt

Cooking Instructions:

1. In a small mixing bowl, stir together all the dried spices. Pat chicken breasts dry. Coat with canola oil, then season them liberally on all sides with the spice mixture.

2. Preheat unit by selecting Air Crisp, set the temperature to 375°F, and setting the time to 5 minutes.

3. Select Start/Stop button to begin. After 5 minutes, add chicken to Cook & Crisp Basket.

4. Close crisping lid. Select Air Crisp, set temperature to 375°F, and set time to 35 minutes.

5. While chicken is cooking, combine the chimichurri ingredients in the bowl of a food processor and process until finely minced, being careful not to over-blend.

6. After 25 minutes, check chicken for doneness. Cooking is complete when internal temperature reaches 165°F.

7. Cook for up to 35 minutes. When cooking is complete, allow chicken to cool for about 5 minutes, then serve with a generous amount of chimichurri.

Cheesy Chicken Crunchadilla

Preparation time: 5 minutes

Cooking time: 20 minutes

Overall time: 25 minutes

Serves: 1 to 3 people

Recipe Ingredients:

- 1 flour tortilla (12 inches)
- 1 cup of cooked chicken meat, shredded, divided
- ½ package (4 ounces) of prepared cheese product, cut in 1/2-inch cubes, divided
- 1 Roma tomato, diced, divided
- 2 scallions, thinly sliced, divided
- 2 corn tostadas, divided
- ¼ cup of shredded Mexican cheese blend

Cooking Instructions:

1. Lay flour tortilla onto a clean surface. Place ½ cup of shredded chicken onto center of tortilla.

2. Sprinkle half of the cubed cheese evenly on top of shredded chicken, then sprinkle with half the tomatoes and half the scallions. Place one tostada on top.

3. Repeat the first step with layers of remaining chicken, cubed cheese, tomatoes, and scallions. Top with second tostada and shredded cheese.

4. Gently fold flour tortilla over the layers in a concentric pattern, about 4 folds, until the crunchadilla is securely wrapped.

5. Using a broken piece of tostada or a torn piece of tortilla, cover the center opening of the crunchadilla so all contents remain secure during cooking.

6. Gently flip crunchadilla over, seam-side down, and coat the top with cooking spray. Place crunchadilla in Cook & Crisp Basket.

7. Select Air Crisp, set temperature to 360°F, and set time to 8 minutes. Select Start/Stop to begin.

8. When cooking is complete, crunchadilla is ready to serve.

Turkey Breast

Preparation time: 10 minutes

Cooking time: 1 hour

Overall time: 1 hour 10 minutes

Serves: 4 to 6 people

Recipe Ingredients

- 3 lb. of boneless turkey breast, thawed
- ½ tablespoon of rosemary
- Olive oil spray

Cooking Instructions:

1. Cut the netting off the turkey breast, place the turkey breast in the basket of the Ninja Foodi.

2. Coat it with olive oil spray and rosemary. Cook at 350°F on air crisp function for about 20 minutes.

3. Carefully turn the turkey breast, coat it again with olive oil spray and a dash of rosemary.

4. Cook for an additional 30 minutes in the air fryer or air crisp function at 350°F. Be sure the internal temperature reaches at least 165°F.

5. Allow it to sit in the Ninja Foodi for about 10 to 15 minutes after cooking to rest. Slice and serve.

Turkey Bone Broth

Preparation time: 30 minutes

Cooking time: 8 hours

Overall time: 8 hours 30 minutes

Serves: 8 to 10 people

Recipe Ingredients:

- Bones of 1 turkey carcass
- Extra seasoning
- 2 tablespoon of olive oil (or avocado oil)
- 10 - 12 cups of cool water

Cooking Instructions:

1. In a large roasting pan, drizzle the oil over the carcass, skin and cartilage.

2. Season with the same seasonings that you used to cook the turkey. Roast in the oven at 350°F for about 30 minutes, until the bones become dark and brittle.

3. Place everything from the roasting pan into the Foodi cooking insert. Add enough water to reach the fill line on the side of the insert.

4. Place the lid on the top, be sure the toggle switch is in the "venting" position, and press slow cook and adjust the time for about 8 hours.

5. After the cooking time is up, seive the contents from the soup through a colander. The broth is ready to be used.

6. Serve immediately and Enjoy!

Frozen Turkey Breast & Mashed Potatoes

Preparation time: 5 minutes

Cooking time: 20 minutes

Overall time: 25 minutes

Serves: 2 to 4 people

Recipe Ingredients:

Turkey Breast:

- 1 (6 lb.) turkey breast bone in
- 1 cup of chicken broth
- 4 tbsp. of butter softened
- Season All (salt & pepper fine as well)

Turkey Gravy:

- 4 tbsp. of unsalted butter
- 3 tbsp. of all-purpose flour
- ½ tsp. of pepper
- 1 cup of turkey drippings
- 1 cup of low-sodium chicken broth

Mashed Potatoes:

- 6 Large Potatoes Peeled and cubed
- 1 cup of chicken broth
- 2 tablespoons of butter
- ¼ cup of milk

Cooking Instructions:

1. Place frozen turkey breast on a trivet inside of your pot. Rub with butter and season well with Season All or salt & pepper. Pour in 1 cup of chicken broth.

2. Close the pressure-cooking lid, make sure it's in the sealing position and turn toggle to seal.

3. Press Pressure set to High pressure and set time to 40 minutes. Hit the Start/Stop button.

4. Once done, do a quick release. Remove the trivet with the turkey breast on it and place it aside. Pour 1 cup of broth from your pot and set aside for gravy.

5. Put potato cubes into your pot. Pressure cook potatoes for 8 minutes. Do a quick release. Remove your potatoes to a bowl for mashing.

6. Put turkey breast back into your pot still on the trivet. Air crisp on 390°F for about 15 minutes or until the skin is nice and golden.

7. Serve immediately and Enjoy!

Turkey Meatloaf

Preparation time: 10 minutes

Cooking time: 30 minutes

Overall time: 40 minutes

Serves: 2 to 4 people

Recipe Ingredients:

- 1/2 cup ketchup
- 1 tablespoon Worcestershire sauce
- 1 tablespoon brown sugar
- 1 teaspoon dry mustard
- 1 1/2 pounds ground turkey
- 2 large shallots, minced
- 1 tablespoon Worcestershire sauce
- 1 tablespoon tomato paste
- 1 egg, lightly beaten
- 2/3 cup bread crumbs (approximately)
- 2 teaspoons granulated garlic
- 2 teaspoons dry mustard
- 2 teaspoons thyme
- Salt & fresh ground pepper (to taste)
- 1 1/2 cups water

Cooking Instructions:

1. In a small bowl, combine ketchup, Worcestershire sauce, brown sugar, and dry mustard and set it aside.

2. In a separate large bowl, add turkey, shallots, Worcestershire sauce, tomato paste, and bread crumbs. Massage with your hands to combine.

3. Season the meat mixture with granulated garlic, dry mustard, thyme, salt and pepper. Massage again to combine. Line an 8″ cake pan with foil.

4. Put the meat mixture into the cake pan. Spread it out to the edges and flatten it until it is even on the top.

5. Add a short steaming rack into the inner pot of your Ninja Foodi. Add the water to the bottom of the Ninja Foodi. Put the meatloaf on top of the steaming rack.

6. Cover the cooker with the pressure lid. Move the vent on the cooker to seal. Use the high-pressure cycle for about 25 minutes.

7. Once the cooker is finished and it changes over to keep warm, allow it to naturally release for about 5 minutes.

8. Release the rest of the pressure. Glaze the top of the meatloaf with the sauce. Put the air fryer lid down.

9. Set the cooker for about air fry to 375 degrees for about 10 minutes. When the glaze is bubbly.

10. Carefully remove the meatloaf from the cooker using a pressure cooker gripper clip.

11. Remove the meatloaf from the cake pan onto a platter using the foil as a sling. Cut and serve. Enjoy!

Rotisserie Roasted Chicken

Preparation time: 10 minutes

Cooking time: 40 minutes

Overall time: 50 minutes

Serves: 2 to 4 people

Recipe Ingredients:

- 1 whole chicken
- 3 tbsp. of olive oil
- 4 tsp. of salt
- 2 tsp. of paprika
- 1 tsp. of onion powder
- 1 teaspoon thyme
- 1 tsp. of white pepper
- ½ tsp. of cayenne pepper
- ½ tsp. of black pepper
- ½ tsp. of garlic powder

Cooking Instructions:

1. Start by cleaning your chicken, remove the package of gizzards, liver, etc. and run water through it, until it comes out clean.

2. Then a small bowl mix all of the spices together. Then rub the oil on one side of the chicken, and the rub mixture.

3. Pour 1 cup of water into the Ninja Foodi, if it does not have water, it will not come to pressure.

4. Put your chicken into the Ninja Foodi Basket, and lock that into the pressure cooker.

5. Use the Pressure cooker lid, and set the time for about 25 minutes on high mode, make sure that the vent is in the sealed position.

6. Press the start button to begin and allow the pressure naturally release, then add more of the rub and olive to the chicken, and put the air fryer lid on.

7. Set for another 10 minutes. When the chicken is done, remove it and let sit, as the juices will distribute through the chicken, as you allow it to cool down. Plate, serve and enjoy!

Bacon Wrapped Chicken

Preparation time: 10 minutes

Cooking time: 10 minutes

Overall time: 20 minutes

Serves: 2 to 4 people

Recipe Ingredients:

- 4 Each boneless, skinless chicken breasts cut into tenderloins
- 12 slices bacon
- ¼ cup of grapeseed oil can substitute vegetable oil
- 1/3 cup of brown sugar
- 2 tbsp. of honey
- 3 cloves of minced garlic
- 1 tsp. of paprika
- ½ tsp. of garlic powder
- ½ tsp. of onion powder
- ¼ tsp. of cayenne pepper
- ¼ tsp. of black pepper
- ¼ tsp. of salt

Cooking Instructions:

1. In a small bowl, mix together all the ingredients except chicken and bacon.

2. Rub the glaze mixture on one side of the chicken breasts. Bacon wrapped chicken wrap each breast in 2-3 slices of bacon.

3. Chicken wrapped in bacon Insert the probe in the Ninja Foodi Grill and preheat to 500°F. Insert the other end of the probe in the largest piece of chicken.

4. Once preheated place chicken on the grill. Chicken on the grill Cook to 100° and then flip over.

5. Continue to cook to 170°F. Baste with additional honey as needed to keep it moist. Serve immediately and Enjoy!

Bayou Cajun-Stuffed Chicken

Preparation time: 5 minutes

Cooking time: 35 minutes

Overall time: 40 minutes

Serves: 2 to 4 people

Recipe Ingredients:

- 2 tbsp. of extra-virgin olive oil
- 1 cup of medium onion, diced
- 1 cup of red and green bell pepper, diced
- ¼ tsp. of Kosher salt
- ¼ tsp. of ground black pepper
- 4 boneless, skinless chicken breasts
- 1 cup of shredded cheddar
- 2 tbsp. of Cajun seasoning

Cooking Instructions:

1. Select Sear/Sauté button and set it to Medium High. Select Start/Stop button to begin. Allow the pot to preheat for about 5 minutes.

2. Add onions and peppers and sauté until the onion is soft about 4 minutes. Remove after cook and set it aside.

3. With a sharp paring knife, cut a pocket in each chicken breast. Stuff each chicken with vegetable mixture, top with cheddar and fold over to close chicken breast.

4. Organize each stuffed chicken breast in the bottom of Ninja Multi-Purpose Pan Season chicken all over with Cajun seasoning, salt, and pepper.

5. Preheat Ninja Foodi on Bake/Roast mode at 325°F, place Ninja Multi-Purpose Pan and bake until cooked through for about 25 minutes.

6. Check with Instant thermometer bake until chicken reaches temperature of 165° internally.

7. Serve immediately and Enjoy!

Whole Chicken Recipe

Preparation time: 20 minutes

Cooking time: 50 minutes

Overall time: 1 hour 10 minutes

Serves: 4 to 6 people

Recipe Ingredients:

- 4 lb. of whole chicken
- ½ tsp. of dried oregano
- ½ tsp. of dried thyme leaves
- ½ tsp. of salt
- ½ tsp. of freshly ground pepper
- 2 cloves of garlic, minced
- 1 bulb of garlic, whole
- 1 ½ cups of water
- 2 tbsp. of butter, melted

Cooking Instructions:

1. Remove any giblets or packets from inside the chicken. Pat the chicken dry. Mix together the oregano, thyme, salt, and pepper.

2. Lift the skin of the chicken and rub minced garlic as well as half the seasoning blend between the skin and the meat of the chicken.

3. Skin being lifted up on a raw whole chicken Put an entire bulb of garlic inside of the chicken. Tie the chicken legs together with cooking twine.

4. Chicken legs tied together with bakers twine. Pour the water into the cooker pot. Place chicken in the crisping basket, tucking the wings under the bird.

5. Cover the cooker with the pressure lid and set the valve to sealing. Set the Ninja Foodi to pressure cook for about 22 minutes.

6. Press start/stop button to begin the cooking cycle. Once the cycle is complete, allow the pressure to naturally release for about 5 minutes before quick release.

7. Brush the chicken with melted butter and sprinkle with remaining dried seasonings.

8. Whole pressure-cooked chicken sprinkled with herbs. Cover with crisping lid and set the Air Crisp function to 400°F.

9. Cook for about 8 minutes. The chicken is done when the meat reaches an internal temperature of 165 degrees.

10. When done, remove chicken from cooker and allow to rest for about 10 minutes before slicing.

Rotisserie Roasted Chicken (Whole Chicken)

Preparation time: 10 minutes

Cooking time: 40 minutes

Overall time: 50 minutes

Serves: 4 to 6 people

Recipe Ingredients:

- 1 whole chicken (about 4 pounds)
- 3 tbsp. of olive oil
- 4 tsp. of salt
- 2 tsp. of paprika
- 1 tsp. of onion powder
- 1 tsp. of thyme
- 1 tsp. of white pepper
- ½ tsp. of cayenne pepper
- ½ tsp. of black pepper
- ½ tsp. of garlic powder

Cooking Instructions:

1. Start by cleaning your chicken, remove the package of heart/gizzards, liver, etc. and run water through it, until it comes out clean.

2. Then a small bowl mix all of the spices together. Then rub the oil on one side of the chicken, and the rub mixture.

3. Pour 1 cup of water into the Ninja Foodi, if it does not have water, it will not come to pressure.

4. Put your chicken into the Ninja Foodi Basket, and lock that into the pressure cooker.

5. Use the Pressure cooker lid, and set the time for about 25 minutes on high mode. Make sure that the vent is in the sealed position.

6. Press the start button, let the pressure naturally release, then add more of the rub and olive to the chicken, and put the air fryer lid on.

7. Set for another 10 minutes. When the chicken is done, remove it and let sit, as the juices will distribute through the chicken, as you allow it to cool down. Plate, serve and enjoy!

Garlic Ranch Chicken Wings

Preparation time: 15 minutes

Cooking time20 minutes

Overall time: 35 minutes

Serves: 1 to 3 people

Recipe Ingredients:

- 1 pound of chicken wings
- 1 tbsp. of ranch seasoning mix
- 1 tbsp. of garlic powder
- 2 tbsp. of mayonnaise

Cooking Instructions:

1. Wash and dry chicken wings with paper towels.

2. Place them in 1 gallon of zip lock bag. Add spices and mayonnaise. Close the bag and shake it. Marinate for at least 15 minutes. Few hours is possible.

3. Open the bag and using thongs place wings in the Ninja Foodi air frying basket. Close the lid and push the Air Crisp button.

4. Cook at 400° F for about 20 minutes. Flip once. If the skin is not crisp enough, cook for additional 5 minutes.

5. Serve immediately and Enjoy!

Rotisserie Chicken

Preparation time: 10 minutes

Cooking time: 45 minutes

Overall time: 55 minutes

Serves: 4 to 6 people

Recipe Ingredients:

- 5 pound of whole pound chicken
- 2 tbsp. of butter, melted
- 1 ½ cups of water
- 3 lemons, zested and halved
- ¼ tsp. of salt
- 1 ½ tsp. of black pepper
- 1 tsp. of onion powder
- ½ tsp. of garlic powder

Cooking Instructions:

1. Start by prepping your bird. Remove giblets and packets inside the chicken. Then with a paper towel or clean towel pat the chicken dry.

2. Now in a small bowl add your lemon zest, salt, pepper, onion powder, and garlic. Lift up the skin on the chicken breast and smear half the rub onto the chicken.

3. Put your lemon halves inside the chicken. Tie the legs with baker's twine. Put water in the cooker pot, and then place chicken in the crisping basket.

4. Tuck wings under the bird. Cover with pressure cooker lid, make sure it is sealed, and then do pressure cooker for about 22 minutes.

5. Naturally release pressure for about 5 minutes, then remove the rest of the pressure.

6. Now with melted butter brush over the top of the chicken and then sprinkle with the rest of the seasoning.

7. Cover with crisping lid and do air crisp function at 400°F for about 8 minutes. Make sure the chicken reaches 165°F internal temperature.

8. If your chicken needs longer go ahead and cook it more. Let chicken rest for 10 minutes on counter before you slice.

Chicken Fajitas

Prep Time: 10 minutes

Cook Time: 24 minutes

Total Time: 34 minutes

Serves: 8 to 10 people

Recipe Ingredients:

- 2 lb. of boneless, skinless chicken thighs
- 1 red bell pepper, diced
- 1 green bell pepper, diced
- ½ cup of sweet onion, diced
- 2 tbsp. of gluten-free fajita or taco seasoning
- Olive oil spray
- Corn and/or flour tortillas

Cooking Instructions:

1. Spray the air fryer basket with olive oil spray. Slice the chicken thighs in bite-size slices.

2. Add the chicken to the basket along with the peppers, onion, and seasoning. Stir to mix it together.

3. Spray evenly with a coat of olive oil cooking spray. Cook at 390°F for about 12 minutes.

4. Halfway through the cooking time, open the lid and stir up the fajita meat, then spray with another coat of olive oil spray.

5. Cook for an additional 12 minutes or until chicken is well done. Serve with warm tortillas.

Shredded Chicken

Preparation time: 5 minutes

Cooking time: 20 minutes

Overall time: 25 minutes

Serves: 4 to 6 people

Recipe Ingredients:

- 2 lb. of chicken breasts
- 1 cup of chicken bone broth
- 1 tsp. of salt
- 2 cups of barbeque sauce

Cooking Instructions:

1. Place the chicken breasts inside of the Ninja Foodi cooking pot and sprinkle with salt. Pour the bone broth over the chicken breasts.

2. Install the pressure-cooking lid and switch the vent knob to seal. Select the pressure cooker function on high and the time to 8 minutes, press the start button to begin.

3. When the timer goes off, quick release the pressure on the Foodi. Carefully remove the lid. Drain the liquid and remove the chicken from the cooking pot.

4. Use two forks to shred the chicken into desired pieces. Stir in the BBQ sauce. Serve with your favorite bread or buns!

Crispy Chicken and Sweet Potatoes

Preparation time: 10 minutes

Cooking time: 45 minutes

Overall time: 55 minutes

Serves: 1 to 3 people

Recipe Ingredients:

Sweet Potatoes:

- 1½ pounds of sweet potatoes cubed
- 1 tablespoon olive oil divided
- 1 teaspoon of salt
- ½ teaspoon of cinnamon

Chicken:

- 1 pound of chicken
- ½ teaspoon of salt
- ¼ teaspoon pepper
- ¼ teaspoon of garlic powder
- 1 tablespoon of olive oil

Cooking Instructions:

1. Wash 1½ pounds of sweet potatoes and cut into cubes about 1-2 inches thick. Place into a bowl. Add olive oil, salt, cinnamon and toss/mix together.

2. Mix with your hands and place the frying rack into the cooking pot of the Ninja Foodi. Make sure it's in the highest position.

3. Place sweet potatoes on rack. You may need to do this in two batches. Turn on the Ninja Foodi and set to Air Crisp at 390°F for about 10 minutes.

4. After 10 minutes, remove rack and add sweet potatoes to basket. Place basket back into the Ninja Foodi.

5. Set to Air Crisp at 390°F for about 10 minutes. Repeat steps 4 and 5 if making multiple batches.

6. Brush chicken on both sides with olive oil. Sprinkle both sides of all the chicken with salt, pepper, and garlic powder.

7. Place frying rack back in the cooking pot of the Ninja Foodi. Rack needs to be in the highest position.

8. Place chicken on the rack in a single layer. Set Ninja Foodi on Air Crisp setting at 390°F.

9. Set for about 30 minutes, depending on thickness and desired crisp. For defrosted chicken, set for 20-25 min depending on thickness and desired crisp.

Spanish Garlic Chicken

Preparation time: 5 minutes

Cooking time: 35 minutes

Overall time: 40 minutes

Serves: 3 to 5 people

Recipe Ingredients:

- 6 chicken thighs with skin
- ¾ cups of butter
- 8 cloves of garlic, 5 whole, 3 sliced very thin
- ¼ chicken broth
- ½ cup of sherry

Cooking Instructions:

1. Put ¼ cup of butter in you pot on sauté mode. Toss in 5 whole garlic cloves. Let it sauté until butter is melted.

2. Pour in ¼ cup of chicken broth. Add in chicken thighs. Continue to saute for a few minutes.

3. Close the pressure-cooking lid, make sure it's in the sealing position and turn toggle to seal. Press Pressure and set to High pressure, set time to 8 minutes.

4. Press the Start button. Once done, do a quick release. Remove the thighs to a plate. Dump ¾ of the leftover liquid.

5. Turn the Sauté mode on. Place your thighs back into your pot. Sprinkle garlic salt over your thighs. Pour ½ cup of melted butter over the thighs.

6. Add in ½ cup of Sherry. Pour in the 3 cloves of sliced garlic. allowing some of the pieces to fall on top of your thighs.

7. Sauté until the garlic pieces are brown and caramelized. Close the crisping lid. Press Air Crisp, time will automatically be set time to 15 minutes.

8. Air Crisp for about 15 minutes. You will want to open your lid and check on your thighs for brownness.

9. Serve with as much of the liquid, garlic gold as your heart desires. Enjoy!

White Chicken Chili

Preparation time: 5 minutes

Cooking time: 25 minutes

Overall time: 30 minutes

Serves: 2 to 4 people

Recipe Ingredients:

- 2 pounds of chicken breast
- 1 tbsp. of minced garlic
- 2 cans (15.5 ounces each) great northern beans, un-drained
- 2 cups of chicken broth
- 1 tsp. of salt
- 1 tsp. of cumin
- ½ tsp. of pepper
- ¼ tsp. of cayenne pepper
- 1 cup of sour cream
- 1/2 cup of whole whipping cream
- Toppings like shredded cheese, diced onion, diced tomatoes, and guacamole
- 1 tablespoon lime and some cilantro (optional)

Cooking Instructions:

1. Add all your ingredients, except the Dairy into your pressure cooker pot.

2. Seal your release. Turn your pressure cooker on High for about 20 minutes. It will take some time to come up to pressure and then the countdown will start.

3. Once its complete, move your seal to Quick Release. Your chicken should be far apart cooked.

4. You can either shred the chicken in the pot with two forks or pull it out with tongs and shred on a cooking board and add back to pot.

5. Now that your chicken and veggies are cooked, add your sour cream and whipping cream and whisk in. Serve with suggested toppings.

Roast Chicken

Preparation time: 5 minutes

Cooking time: 40 minutes

Overall time: 45 minutes

Serves: 2 to 4 people

Recipe Ingredients:

- 4 lb. of whole chicken
- 5 cloves of garlic, peeled and crushed
- ¾ cup of hot water
- 2 tbsp. of butter, melted
- Parsley for garnish, optional

Cooking Instructions:

1. Clean chicken and pat dry. Set aside. Place garlic and water in Ninja Foodi pot. Sprinkle chicken generously with dry rub or own seasonings.

2. Make sure to season the inside of chicken as well as under skin. Set Cook & Crisp Basket in pot and place chicken in basket breast side up.

3. Assemble pressure lid, making sure the pressure release valve is in the SEAL position.

4. Select Pressure and set to high mode for about 21 minutes. When pressure cooking is complete, allow to natural release for about 15 minutes.

5. Carefully remove lid when pressure has been released. Brush chicken with melted butter and lightly sprinkle with a bit more seasoning.

6. Close the crisping lid and Air Crisp at 400°F for about 20 minutes. Let chicken rest for about 10 minutes.

7. Ensure its internal temperature reaches 165 degrees Fahrenheit. Serve immediately and Enjoy!

Garlic and Parm crusted chicken with roasted potatoes

Preparation time: 5 minutes

Cooking time: 30 minutes

Overall time: 35 minutes

Serves: 1 to 3 people

Recipe Ingredients:

- 5 lb. of cubed potatoes
- 1 lb. of chicken breast
- 1.5 sticks of butter
- 1 cup of panko bread crumbs
- 1 egg
- 1 tablespoon of Italian seasonings
- ½ cup of shredded Parm cheese
- 1 tablespoon of garlic powder
- ½ tablespoon of salt
- ½ tablespoon of pepper

Cooking Instructions:

1. Melt butter. Stir in garlic powder and Italian seasonings. Place chopped potatoes in the bottom of your Ninja Foodi.

2. Pour butter over the potatoes making sure they are all coated well. Mix together panko and parm cheese.

3. Whisk your Egg and dip chicken breast in egg then in panko Mix. Place a trivet on top of your potatoes. Place your chicken breast on top of the trivet.

4. Cook on manual high pressure for about 10 minutes. Do a Quick Release Remove the pressure lid and cook on air fry 390 for about 15 minutes.

5. If you don't have the ninja remove your chicken and place in the broiler for about 5 minutes. Serve and enjoy!

BEEF, PORK AND LAMB RECIPES

Barbeque Beef Short Ribs

Preparation time: 10 minutes

Cooking time: 40 minutes

Overall time: 50 minutes

Serves: 2 to 4 people

Recipe Ingredients:

- 2 beef short ribs
- ¼ cup of red wine
- ¾ cup of beef stock
- ¼ cup of diced onion
- ½ cup of barbeque sauce

Seasoning as desired:

- Seasoning salt
- Garlic powder
- Onion powder
- 1 tablespoon of cornstarch

Cooking Instructions:

1. Season the beef ribs with the seasonings above. Add the onion, wine, and broth to the bottom of the Foodi cooking bowl.

2. Close the toggle switch to sealing Pressure cook on manual, high mode, for about 40 minutes.

3. Do a natural pressure release for about 10 minutes, and then carefully release any remaining pressure until the pin drops and it is safe to open the lid.

4. Remove the ribs to a plate. Generously brush the barbeque sauce over the entire surface of the ribs.

5. Place the ribs back into the pot, on the top rack of the air crisping rack. Air crisp the ribs for about 10 minutes, watching them closely so as not to burn.

6. Feel free to flip them halfway through. Remove the ribs to rest and take out the rack. Mix up the slurry and pour into the pan juices in the pot to thicken.

7. Spoon over the ribs and enjoy!

Roast Recipe

Preparation time: 15 minutes

Cooking time: 1 hour

Overall time: 1 hour 15 minutes

Serves: 6 to 8 people

Recipe Ingredients:

- 5.8 pounds of Sirloin Roast
- 12 ounces of Cola
- 1 packet of French onion soup mix
- 1 packet of Gravy mix
- 1 can of cream of mushroom soup
- 2 teaspoons of garlic salt
- 3 tablespoons of cornstarch
- 3 tablespoons of cold water
- 1 tablespoon of soy sauce

Cooking Instructions:

1. Whisk together your cola, onion soup mix, dry gravy mix packet, soy sauce and garlic salt so it is lumpy but mixed well.

2. Remove string ties from roast. Slice your roast into 4 equal pieces and put inside your Ninja Foodi.

3. Pour soup mixture on top of roast so it is well coated. Close your pressure cooker lid for Ninja Foodi that isn't connected and close your steam valve.

4. Push your pressure cook button, high mode for about 60 minutes Press the start button to begin.

5. Allow to naturally release completely, then open your lid. To make a thicker gravy remove your meat and set your pot to sauté.

6. In a small bowl whisk together 1/2 cup of the hot liquid in your pot plus a can of condensed soup.

7. Add this into your pot and allow to bubble. If you want it thicker whisk in a bowl 2 tablespoon of cornstarch and 3 tablespoons of cold water until smooth.

8. Add into your pot once it begins to bubble. Keep in mind it will thicken a lot once it cools and sits. Taste gravy as it is thickening and add more salt if desired.

Pulled Pork

Preparation time: 5 minutes

Cooking time: 25 minutes

Overall time: 30 minutes

Serves: 4 to 6 people

Recipe Ingredients:

- 1 pound of pork tenderloin
- 1 tablespoon of olive oil
- ½ tablespoon of paprika
- ½ tablespoon of dry mustard
- 1 teaspoon of kosher salt
- 1 teaspoon of black pepper
- ½ teaspoon of cumin
- 1 tablespoon of swerve brown (or brown sugar)
- ¾ cup (180ml) of low sodium chicken broth
- ¾ cup (192g) barbeque sauce, divided
- 2 tablespoons (30g) of hot sauce (optional)

Cooking Instructions:

1. Mix the salt, pepper, paprika, dry mustard, cumin, and brown sugar together in a small bowl.

2. Mix the chicken broth, ¼ cup (64g) of barbeque sauce, and optional hot sauce in another bowl and set it aside. Rub or brush the olive oil on the pork tenderloin.

3. Coat both sides of the pork tenderloin with the mixed spices. Turn the Foodi's sauté function on High mode.

4. Once the pot is hot, add the pork tenderloin and cook for 2 minutes to develop a good sear on one side. Flip and cook for another 2 minutes.

5. Add the broth mixture, seal the Foodi, and pressure cook on High mode for about 10 to 12 minutes with quick release pressure.

6. Transfer the cooked pork tenderloin to a large bowl to rest. Shredding, Saucing, and Crisping.

7. Turn the Foodi' to sauté function on High mode until the remaining liquid has thickened to a sauce that leaves a trail when you drag a spatula across the pot, for about 5 to 6 minutes.

8. Shred the pork tenderloin with two forks, meat claws, or stand mixer with a paddle attachment.

9. Pour the remaining ½ cup (128g) of Barbeque sauce and stir before adding back to the Foodi with the thickened sauce.

10. Stir to fully coat the pulled pork in the sauces. Use the Foodi's broil function for about 10 to 12 minutes to make the pulled pork crispy.

Grill Juicy Grilled Pork Chops

Preparation time: 5 minutes

Cooking time: 30 minutes

Overall time: 35 minutes

Serves: 2 to 4 people

Recipe Ingredients:

- 4 Pork Chops, bone in or boneless
- Pork Marinade

Cooking Instructions:

1. Make the pork marinade in advance and get your pork chops marinating in the refrigerator before cooking.

2. Insert removable cooking pot. Insert grill grate into your pot. Press grill button, set to high mode at 500°F and set time to 15 minutes.

3. Add pork chops onto grill, close lid and grill for about 7 to 8 minutes, then flip the meat, closing grill once again.

4. Cook for another 5 minutes and check internal temperature to see if has reached an internal temperature of 150 degrees.

5. Allow meat to rest 5 minutes before cutting and serving.

Asian Pulled Pork

Preparation time: 15 minutes

Cooking time: 1 hour 40 minutes

Overall time: 1 hour 55 minutes

Serves: 4 to 6 people

Recipe Ingredients:

- 3 cups of water
- 1 cup of rice wine vinegar
- ¼ cup of sugar
- 1 ½ teaspoons of red pepper flakes divided
- ½ tablespoon of sea salt
- 2 ½ pounds of pork shoulder boneless
- ¼ cup of red peppers diced
- 1 teaspoon of ginger grated (about 1 inch of ginger)
- 1 teaspoon of garlic minced (about 3 cloves)
- 1 ½ tablespoon of honey
- 1 tablespoon of red chili pepper paste
- ¼ cup of orange juice 1 medium orange squeezed

Pickled Vegetables:

- ½ cup of water
- 1/2 cup of rice vinegar
- 1 tablespoon of sugar
- 1-inch ginger sliced thin
- ½ red onion thinly sliced
- 1 carrot cut into matchsticks
- 1 red pepper thinly sliced

Cooking Instructions:

1. Combine water, rice vinegar, sugar, 1 teaspoon of red pepper flakes and ½ tablespoon of sea salt in the inner pot of the Ninja Foodi.

2. Place in pork shoulder. Put the pressure lid on and turn the black valve to seal. Set the time for about 90 minutes.

3. When the time is up, quickly release the remaining pressure. Strain liquid from the pork, reserve ½ cup of liquid.

4. Remove any large pieces of fat from the pork and shred. Put the pork back into the inner pot.

5. Add the ½ cup of the reserved liquid, 1 teaspoon of grated ginger, 1 teaspoon of minced garlic, 1 ½ tablespoons of honey, 1 tablespoon of Red Chili Pepper Paste, and ¼ cup of fresh sqeezed orange juice.

6. Turn the Ninja Foodi on the sear/sauté function and allow to simmer on medium heat for about 10 minutes.

7. Serve on a roll or steamed bun topped with pickled veggies. Enjoy!

Ranch Pork Chops

Preparation time: 5 minutes

Cooking time: 10 minutes

Overall time: 15 minutes

Serves: 2 to 4 people

Recipe Ingredients:

- 1 tbsp. of extra virgin olive oil
- 4-6 Pork chops, thick
- 1 stick of butter, unsalted
- 1 package of Ranch Seasoning
- 1 cup of chicken broth
- Salt
- Pepper
- 1 package of Idahoan Instant Potatoes of Choice
- 1 package Frozen Veggie of Choice

Cooking Instructions:

1. Start your Ninja Foodi to saute mode and add the 1 tablespoon of extra virgin olive oil.

2. When the oil is glistening it's hot. While the oil is heating up, generously salt and pepper your pork chops.

3. Brown both sides of the pork chops in the Ninja Foodi when the oil is hot. Depending on how big your pork chops are you may need to do this in batches.

4. The browning will take a few minutes for each side. Once all your pork chops are browned turn the sauté mode off.

5. Add the chicken broth to the Ninja Foodi. Then sprinkle the Ranch dressing mix over the pork chops and place the stick of butter on top.

6. Place the pressure-cooking lid on the Ninja Foodi and be sure the vent is set to the sealed position. Set to Pressure Cook, high mode for about 5 minutes.

7. When the time is up, let the pressure do a natural release for about 5 minutes then finish with a quick release for the remainder.

8. While the pork chops are cooking, start those taters. Prepare the Idohan potatoes per the box directions.

9. Steam the veggies in the microwave. When the pork chops are done scoop some of the butter ranch sauce and mix it into the potatoes.

10. Drizzle it over the vegetables if you would like. This dinner is a hit! Full of flavor but not full of work.

Bacon Wrapped Tenderloin

Preparation time: 5 minutes

Cooking time: 16 minutes

Overall time: 21 minutes

Serves: 4 to 6 people

Recipe Ingredients:

- 2 pounds of pork tenderloin
- ½ pound of bacon
- 1 teaspoon of salt more or less to taste.
- 1 teaspoon of pepper more or less to taste.
- 1 cup of water

Cooking Instructions:

1. Season the Pork tenderloin with salt and pepper to taste. Wrap tenderloin in bacon.

2. Make sure all bacon ends meet on the same side creating a seam you can lat the pork on.

3. Bacon wrapped pork tenderloin If making potatoes or rice at the same time Either us pot-in-pot method or cover with aluminum foil to capture the pork drippings.

4. Pork with potatoes Place the cup of water in the Ninja Foodi. Lay the pork tenderloins in a circular pattern on the rack and placed in the Ninja Foodi.

5. Place the rack in the low setting, this will prevent having to flip the rack in a future step. Set the Ninja Foodi to Pressure and High mode for about 4 minutes.

6. You will be Air Crisping as well, so do not want to overcook. If you prefer your pork rarer, cook for about 2-3 minutes.

7. Once complete release the pressure. Pull out the potatoes or rice if in the pot. Flip the rack to the low position if needed.

8. place the pork tenderloin back in the Ninja Foodi. Pork cooked and ready to air fry Set the Ninja Foodi to Air Crisp on High mode for about 10 minutes.

9. Depending on how crispy you want the bacon, and how fatty it is you may need to cook longer.

Teriyaki pork tenderloin

Preparation time: 5 minutes

Cooking time: 30 minutes

Overall time: 35 minutes

Serves: 6 to 8 people

Recipe Ingredients:

- 1 14 fluid ounces of teriyaki marinade
- 1 small can of pineapple chunks with juice
- 3 stalks of green scallions
- 2 pork of tenderloins (approx. 2-3 lbs)
- Potato rolls optional

Cooking Instructions:

1. Remove tenderloin from packaging and set in the crisping basket of Ninja Foodi. Add one cup of water to the pot.

2. Pour half the teriyaki sauce on top of the pork tenderloins. Set pot on Pressure cook for about 25 minutes.

3. Let the pressure release naturally. Carefully open pot and add the remaining teriyaki sauce, pineapple chunks and juice on top.

4. Set your Foodi on Broil for approximately 7 minutes. Remove crisper basket, and on a plate, shred tenderloins with a fork.

5. Add back to the foodi in all the sauce, stir and serve. Cut the scallions to add on top for color, little bit of extra texture and flavor. Enjoy!

Baby Back Pork Ribs

Preparation time: 5 minutes

Cooking time: 40 minutes

Overall time: 45 minutes

Serves: 3 to 5 people

Recipe Ingredients

- 1 rack of back ribs; about 3 pounds
- Rib rub
- Barbeque sauce; has a bit of a kick

Cooking Instructions:

1. Rinse ribs and pat dry with a paper towel. Cur the rack into 3 even sections. Remove the membrane from the bone side of the ribs and place on a baking sheet.

2. Generously sprinkle the ribs with the rib rub and gently rub on both sides, place baking sheet with ribs covered with aluminum foil in the refrigerator.

3. Remove ribs from refrigerator and let stand and come to room temperature. Place 1 cup of water into the Foodie inner pot.

4. Place the reversible rack Covered with aluminum foil and slits cut between some of the grates in the pot in the lower position.

5. Place the ribs on the rack, bone side down. Lock the Pressure Lid into place, making sure the valve is set to Seal.

6. Select Pressure; adjust the pressure to High and the cook time to 18 minutes. Press the Start button.

7. After cooking, use a quick pressure release. Carefully unlock and remove the Pressure Lid.

8. Remove the rack and ribs from the inner pot and empty the water out of the pot. Return the inner pot to the base.

9. Place the Reversible Rack with the ribs back in the pot in the lower position. Close the Crisping Lid and select Air Crisp.

10. Adjust the temperature to 400 F and the cook time to 20 minutes. Press Start. After 10 minutes, open the lid and turn the ribs over.

11. Baste the bone side of the ribs with the sauce and close the lid to continue cooking. After 4 minutes, open the lid and turn the ribs again.

12. Baste the meat side of the ribs with additional sauce and close the lid to continue cooking until done.

Shepherd's Pie

Preparation time: 5 minutes

Cooking time: 27 minutes

Overall time: 32 minutes

Serves: 8 to 10 people

Recipe Ingredients:

- ½ bulb of garlic roasted see post for recipe
- 2 pounds of potatoes russet preferred
- 3 cups of beef broth
- 3 ounces of bacon thick cut preferred, diced
- ½ onion sweet onion
- 1.5 pounds of ground beef
- 3 carrots
- 1 cup of corn frozen or canned
- 1 cup of peas frozen
- 1.5 tablespoons of Worcestershire Sauce
- ½ cup of flour

Spice Blend:

- 1 teaspoon of sea salt fine grind
- ½ teaspoon of pepper if you like pepper increase to 1 tsp
- ½ teaspoon of rosemary dried, crushed leaves
- 1 teaspoon of thyme dried

For the Mashed Potatoes:

- ½ teaspoon of sea salt fine grind
- ¼ cup of butter salted
- ¼ cup of heavy whipping cream
- ½ bulb of garlic roasted

Cheese Topping:

- 1 cup of cheddar cheese sharp white, grated
- 1 cup of cheddar cheese sharp yellow, grated
- ½ cup of Asiago grated

Cooking Instructions:

1. Chop up the bacon and, peel and slice the carrots, and dice the onion. Shred the cheese if not using pre-shredded.

2. Peel and chop the potatoes into medium sized pieces. Mix up your seasoning mix. Add the potatoes and beef broth to the inner pot of the Ninja Foodi.

3. Set to high pressure for 10 minutes. Make sure to turn the valve to seal. When done, immediate release and strain the potatoes in a colander.

4. Reserve the beef broth and gently break apart the potato chunks to allow the steam to escape and set it aside.

5. Turn the Ninja Foodi on and set to high sauté. Allow to heat up for a minute or two and add bacon and diced onions.

6. Sauté, stirring occasionally, until the bacon starts to render its fat and the onions begin to cook.

7. Add in the ground beef, seasoning blend, ½ of the bulb of roasted garlic, and the Worcestershire sauce.

8. Continue to sauté until ¾ of the way done, breaking the meat up as you stir. Add Sliced Carrots.

9. Continue to cook meat mixture for about 5 minutes or until carrots are just becoming soft. Add in Frozen Peas and Frozen Corn.

10. Stir to combine, sprinkle on 1/4 cup of flour and stir to incorporate. Repeat with the remaining ¼ cup of flour and cook for about 2 minutes.

11. Slowly add in the beef stock, about 1 cup at a time. Stir until the flour has absorbed most of the stock before adding the next cup. Repeat until all three cups are used.

12. Be sure to scrape the bottom of the Ninja Foodi to remove the browned bits, they add tons of flavor to the sauce.

13. Reduce the heat to medium sauté and cook until thickened. While that is happening, mash your potatoes.

14. Keep an eye on the ground beef mixture and if it is boiling, reduce the heat to low. Mash the potatoes either by and or with a hand mixer.

15. Add remaining ½ bulb of roasted garlic and 1/4 cup of heavy cream, 1/4 cup of butter and ½ teaspoon of salt.

16. Turn the Ninja Foodi off. Layer the mashed potatoes on top of the ground beef mixture.

17. Top with shredded cheese. Air Crisp on 375° F for about 10 to 15 minutes or until the cheese is melted and bubbly. Serve and Enjoy!

Tex-Mex Meatloaf

Preparation time: 15 minutes

Cooking time: 30 minutes

Overall time: 45 minutes

Serves: 6 to 8 people

Recipe Ingredients:

- 1 lb. of uncooked ground beef
- 1 egg
- 1 bell pepper, diced
- ½ jalapeño pepper, seeds removed, minced
- 1 small onion, peeled, diced
- 3 corn tortillas, roughly chopped
- 1 tbsp. of garlic powder
- 2 tsp. of ground cumin
- 2 tsp. of chili powder
- 1 tsp. of cayenne pepper
- 2 tsp. of kosher salt
- ¼ cup of fresh cilantro leaves
- ¼ barbecue sauce, divided
- 1 cup of water
- 1 cup of corn chips, crushed

Cooking Instructions:

1. Stir together beef, egg, bell pepper, jalapeño pepper, onion, tortillas, spices, cilantro, and tablespoons barbecue sauce in a large mixing bowl.

2. Place meat mixture in the loaf pan (or an 8 ½-inch loaf pan) and cover tightly with aluminum foil.

3. Pour water into pot and place the loaf pan on the reversible rack, making sure rack is in the lower position.

4. Place rack with pan in pot and assemble the pressure lid, making sure the Pressure Release valve is in the Seal position.

5. Select Pressure and set to High. Set time to 15 minutes. Select Start/Stop button to begin.

6. When pressure cooking is complete, quick release the pressure by moving the Pressure Release valve to the Vent position.

7. Carefully remove lid when unit has finished releasing pressure. Carefully remove foil from loaf pan and close crisping lid.

8. Select Bake/Roast function, set temperature to 360°F, and set time to 15 minutes. Select Start/Stop button to begin.

9. While the meatloaf is cooking, stir together the crushed corn chips and 2 tablespoons of barbecue sauce in a bowl.

10. After 7 minutes, open lid and top meatloaf with the corn chip mixture. Close lid to resume cooking.

11. When cooking is complete, remove meatloaf from pot and allow to cool for 10 minutes before serving.

Steak, Mashed Potatoes & Asparagus

Preparation time: 10 minutes

Cooking time: 15 minutes

Overall time: 25 minutes

Serves: 2 to 4 people

Recipe Ingredients:

- 5 Russet potatoes, peeled, cut in 1/2-inch pieces
- ½ cup of water
- ¼ cup of butter, divided
- ½ cup of heavy cream
- 1 cup of shredded cheddar cheese
- 1 tbsp. of kosher salt, divided
- 3 tsp. of ground black pepper, divided
- 2 frozen New York strip steaks (12 ounces each, 1 1/2 inches thick)
- 1 bunch of asparagus, trimmed
- 1 tbsp. of olive oil

Cooking Instructions:

1. Place potatoes and water into the pot. Place the reversible rack in the pot over potatoes, making sure rack is in the higher position.

2. Season steaks with 1 tablespoon salt and 1 teaspoon pepper, then place them on the rack.

3. Assemble pressure lid, making sure the Pressure Release valve is in Sealing position. Select Pressure and set to high mode and set time to 1 minute.

4. Select the Start/Stop button to begin. While the unit is pressure cooking, toss the asparagus with olive oil, 1 teaspoon salt, and 1 teaspoon black pepper.

5. When pressure cooking is complete, quick release the pressure by moving the Pressure Release valve to the Vent position.

6. Carefully remove lid when unit has finished releasing pressure. Remove rack with steaks from pot and pat steaks dry.

7. Mash potatoes with ¼ cup of butter, cream, cheese, 1 teaspoon salt, and 1 teaspoon pepper, using a mashing utensil that won't scratch the nonstick surface of the pot.

8. Return rack with steaks to pot over mashed potatoes. Place asparagus on rack next to steaks.

9. Close crisping lid and select Broil and set time to 8 minutes for medium steak or 12 minutes for well-done, elect the Start/Stop button to begin.

10. When cooking is complete, remove steaks from rack and allow to rest for about 5 minutes before serving with mashed potatoes and asparagus.

Pulled Pork with Crispy Biscuits

Preparation time: 10 minutes

Cooking time: 55 minutes

Overall time: 1 hour 5 minutes

Serves: 6 to 8 people

Recipe Ingredients:

- 3 lb. of uncooked boneless pork shoulder, fat trimmed, cut in 2-inch cubes
- 3 tbsp. of barbecue seasoning
- 1 tbsp. of garlic powder
- 2 tsp. of kosher salt
- 1 cup of apple cider vinegar
- 1 can (6 ounces) of tomato paste
- 1 tube (16.3 ounces) of refrigerated biscuit dough

Cooking Instructions:

1. Place pork, spices, and vinegar in the pot. Assemble pressure lid, making sure the Pressure Release valve is in Sealing position.

2. Select Pressure and set to High mode. Set time to 35 minutes and select the Start/Stop button to begin.

3. When pressure cooking is complete, quick release the pressure by moving the Pressure Release valve to the Vent position.

4. Carefully remove lid when unit has finished releasing pressure. Select Sear/Sauté and set to mid :High.

5. Select the Start/Stop button to begin. Add tomato paste and stir to incorporate. Allow pork to simmer for about 10 minutes, or until the liquid has reduced by half.

6. Stir occasionally, using a wooden spoon or silicone tongs to shred the pork. Tear each uncooked biscuit so that it is in two halves, like a hamburger bun.

7. Place biscuit halves evenly across the surface of the pork. Close crisping lid. Select Bake/Roast, set temperature to 350°F, and set time to 10 minutes.

8. Check after 8 minutes, cooking for an additional 2 minutes if biscuits need more browning. When cooking is complete, serve immediately.

Beef Jerky

Preparation time: 15 minutes

Cooking time: 7 hours

Overall time: 7 hours 15 minutes

Serves: 2 to 4 people

Recipe Ingredients:

- ¼ cup of soy sauce
- 2 tbsp. of Worcestershire sauce
- 2 tbsp. of dark brown sugar
- 1 tsp. of ground black pepper
- 1 tsp. of garlic powder
- 1 tsp. of onion powder
- 1 tsp. of paprika
- 2 tsp. of kosher salt
- 1 ½ lb. (24 ounces) uncooked beef eye of round, cut in 1/4-inch slices

Cooking Instructions:

1. Whisk together all ingredients, except beef. place mixture into a large resealable plastic bag.

2. Place sliced beef in bag with seasonings and rub to coat. marinate in refrigerator for at least 8 hours or overnight.

3. strain meat; discard excess liquid. Lay meat slices flat on the ninja dehydrating rack or ninja cook & crisp layered insert.

4. Arrange them in a single layer, without any slices touching each another. Place dehydrating rack or cook & crisp layered insert in cook & crisp basket.

5. Place basket in pot and close crisping lid. press dehydrate, set temperature to 155°f, and set time to 7 hours.

6. Select the start/stop button to begin. jerky will be pliable and soft after 5 hours, continue cooking for up to 7 hours if crispier jerky is desired.

7. When cooking is complete, remove dehydrating rack or cook & crisp layered insert from pot. transfer jerky to an airtight container.

Beef Chili & Cornbread Casserole

Preparation time: 20 minutes

Cooking time: 45 minutes

Overall time: 1 hour 5 minutes

Serves: 6 to 8 people

Recipe Ingredients:

- 2 lb. of uncooked ground beef
- 3 cans (14 oz. each) of kidney beans, rinsed, drained
- 1 can (28 ounces) of crushed tomatoes
- 1 cup of beef stock
- 1 large white onion, peeled, diced
- 1 green bell pepper, diced
- 1 jalapeño pepper, diced, seeds removed
- 4 cloves of garlic, peeled, minced
- 2 tbsp. of kosher salt
- 1 tbsp. of ground black pepper
- 2 tbsp. of ground cumin
- 1 tbsp. of onion powder
- 1 tasp. garlic powder
- 2 cups of Cheddar Corn Bread batter, uncooked (see recipe page 61)
- 1 cup of shredded Mexican cheese blend
- Sour cream, for serving

Cooking Instructions:

1. Place beef, beans, tomatoes, and stock into the pot, breaking apart meat.

2. Assemble pressure lid, making sure the pressure release valve is in the seal position. Select pressure and set to high. Set time to 15 minutes.

3. Select the start/stop button to begin. When pressure cooking is complete, quick release the pressure by moving the pressure release valve to the vent position.

4. Carefully remove lid when unit has finished releasing pressure. Select sear/sauté and set to mid high mode and select the start/stop button.

5. Add onion, green bell pepper, jalapeño pepper, garlic, and spices; stir to incorporate. Bring to a simmer and cook for 5 minutes, stirring occasionally.

6. Dollop corn bread batter evenly over the top of the chili. Close crisping lid. Select bake/roast, set temperature to 360°F, and set time to 26 minutes.

7. Select start/stop to begin. After 15 minutes, open lid and insert a wooden toothpick into the center of the corn bread.

8. If toothpick comes out clean, skip to step 7. If corn bread is not done, close lid to resume cooking for another 8 minutes.

9. When corn bread is done, sprinkle it with cheese and close lid to resume cooking for 3 minutes, or until cheese is melted.

10. When cooking is complete, top with sour cream and serve.

Lamb Shanks with Roasted Carrots

Preparation time: 10 minutes

Cooking time: 55 minutes

Overall time: 1 hour 5 minutes

Serves: 2 to 4 people

Recipe Ingredients:

- 3 tbsp. of olive oil, divided
- 4 lamb shanks (about 3 lb. total)
- 2 tsp. of kosher salt, plus more for seasoning
- 2 tsp. of paprika
- 1 tsp. of ground cumin
- 1 tsp. of ground cinnamon
- 1 tsp. of ground black pepper
- 1 cup of red wine
- 2 cloves of garlic, peeled
- 1 lb. of baby carrots
- 1 tbsp. of instant flour

Cooking Instructions:

1. Add 2 tablespoons olive oil to the pot. Select the sear/sauté button and set to high. Select the start/stop button to begin.

2. Allow it to preheat for 5 minutes. After 5 minutes, add lamb shanks to pot. Sear until browned on all sides, for about 10 minutes.

3. Add salt and spices to the pot and cook until aromatic, stirring, about one minute. Add the red wine and garlic to the pot.

4. Scrape the bottom for any browned bits. Assemble pressure lid, making sure the pressure release valve is in the seal position.

5. Select pressure and set to high and set time to 15 minutes. Select the start/stop button to begin.

6. When pressure cooking is complete, quick release the pressure by moving the pressure release valve to the vent position.

7. Carefully remove lid when unit has finished releasing pressure. Place the reversible rack in the pot over shanks, making sure rack is in the higher position.

8. Place carrots on rack. Assemble pressure lid, making sure the pressure release valve is in the seal position. Select pressure and set to high. Set time to 10 minutes.

9. Select the start/stop button to begin. When pressure cooking is complete, quick release the pressure by moving the pressure release valve to the vent position.

10. Carefully remove lid when unit has finished releasing pressure. Drizzle 1 tablespoon olive oil over the carrots.

11. Season the carrots with a pinch of salt, then close the crisping lid. Select broil and set time to 10 minutes. Select start/stop to begin.

12. When cooking is complete, remove carrots and lamb shanks from the pot and allow to rest. Select sear/sauté and set to high. Select start/stop to begin.

13. Add instant flour to the liquid in the pot, whisking constantly. Bring mixture to a boil. Once boiling, press the power button to turn off sear/sauté.

14. Ladle the sauce over the lamb and serve.

Stuffed Grape Leaves

Preparation time: 40 minutes

Cooking time: 12 minutes

Overall time: 52 minutes

Serves: 8 to 10 people

Recipe Ingredients:

- 1 cup of uncooked basmati rice
- 2 lb. of ground beef or lamb
- 4 cloves of garlic, peeled, minced
- ¼ cup of fresh parsley, chopped
- ¼ cup of fresh mint, chopped
- 2 tsp. of allspice
- 2 tsp. of onion powder
- 1 tsp. of kosher salt
- ½ tsp. of pepper
- 1 jar (15 oz.) of grape leaves
- ½ cup of lemon juice
- ½ cup of water

Cooking Instructions:

1. Mix basmati rice, ground meat, garlic, herbs, and spices together in a large bowl. Rinse jarred grape leaves under cool water and separate onto paper towels.

2. Cover the bottom of the pot with a few plain grape leaves. On paper towels or a cutting board, carefully spread out one grape leaf at a time, vein side up.

3. Remove the stem, start by adding 1 tablespoon meat filling at the bottom of the leaf. The amount of filling will determine the size of each grape leaf.

4. Fold the edges in and up, then roll the grape leaf until it looks like a cigar, tucking the edges under the roll. Repeat with remaining grape leaves.

5. Place rolled grape leaves in the pot, packing them together tightly and facing them in the same direction.

6. Once you've finished placing the first layer, place the second layer in the opposite direction. After all the grapes leaves are placed in the pot.

7. Add water and lemon juice. Assemble pressure lid, making sure the pressure release valve is in the seal position. Select pressure and set to high.

8. Set time to 12 minutes. Select the start/stop button to begin. When cooking is complete, allow pressure to natural release for about 10 minutes.

9. After 10 minutes, quick release any remaining pressure by moving the pressure release valve to the vent position.

10. Carefully remove lid when unit has finished releasing pressure. Let the grape leaves cool slightly before transferring to a platter and serving.

Corned Beef Hash

Preparation time: 15 minutes

Cooking time: 35 minutes

Overall time: 50 minutes

Serves: 4 to 6 people

Recipe Ingredients:

- ½ lb. of cooked corned beef, diced
- 2 tbsp. of vegetable oil
- 1 white onion, peeled, finely chopped
- 1 bell pepper, finely chopped
- 2 medium baking potatoes, peeled, diced
- ½ tsp. of ground black pepper
- 3 tsp. of kosher salt, divided
- 6 large eggs
- Hot sauce, for serving

Cooking Instructions:

1. Select the sear/sauté button and set to high mode. Select start/stop to begin. Allow to preheat for about 5 minutes.

2. Add corned beef to pot and sauté for about 5 minutes, or until fat has rendered. Add oil, onion, pepper, and potatoes to pot.

3. Season with pepper and 2 teaspoons salt. Sauté for about 5 to 10 minutes, until onions are translucent and peppers have softened.

4. Then let the onions and peppers cook for another 5 minutes, without stirring, so that a crust forms on the bottom.

5. After 5 minutes, stir mixture. Then let cook for another 5 minutes, without stirring. Crack eggs onto the surface on the hash and season with remaining salt.

6. Close the crisping lid. Select broil and set time to 10 minutes. Check eggs frequently, cooking until desired doneness.

7. When cooking is complete, serve eggs and hash immediately with hot sauce.

Beef Stew Pot Pie

Preparation time: 20 minutes

Cooking time: 40 minutes

Overall time: 1 hour

Serves: 4 to 6 people

Recipe Ingredients:

- 2 tbsp. of olive oil
- 1 onion, peeled, diced
- 1 stalk celery, diced
- 2 carrots, peeled, cut in 1/2-inch cubes
- 2 cloves of garlic, peeled, minced
- 2 lb. of uncooked sirloin steaks or stew meat, cut in 1/2-inch cubes
- 1 tsp. of dried thyme
- 2 tsp. of kosher salt
- 1 tsp. of pepper
- 2 russet potatoes, peeled, cut in 1/2-inch cubes
- 2 cups of beef stock
- 2 tbsp. of Worcestershire sauce
- ½ cup of frozen peas, thawed
- ¼ cup of quick-thickening flour
- 1 store-bought refrigerated pie crust, room temperature

Cooking Instructions:

1. Select the sear/sauté button and set to mid high. Select start/stop to begin. Allow to preheat for about 5 minutes.

2. After 5 minutes, add oil, onion, celery, carrots, and garlic to the pot. Cook until softened, stirring occasionally, for about 5 minutes.

3. Add meat and cook until browned on all sides, about 3 minutes. Add seasonings, potatoes, stock, and Worcestershire sauce.

4. Stir to combine and select the start/stop button to turn off sear/sauté function. Assemble pressure lid.

5. Make sure the pressure release valve is in the seal position. Select pressure and set to high. Set time to 20 minutes.

6. Select the start/stop button to begin. When pressure cooking is complete, quick release the pressure by moving the pressure release valve to the vent position.

7. Carefully remove lid when unit has finished releasing pressure. Select sear/sauté function and set to mid high.

8. Select the start/stop button to begin. Let stew come to a simmer, then add peas to pot. Add flour to the pot and slowly stir into stew.

9. Allow stew to thicken, then select the start/stop button to turn off sear/sauté function.

10. Lay the pie dough evenly over the top of the mixture, folding the edges under. Close crisping lid. Select broil and set time to 10 minutes.

11. Select the start/stop button to begin. Cooking is complete when pie crust is golden brown. Let it rest for about 5 minutes before serving.

Beef Barley Soup

Preparation time: 15 minutes

Cooking time: 25 minutes

Overall time: 40 minutes

Serves: 4 to 6 people

Recipe Ingredients:

- 1 tbsp. of canola oil
- 2 ½ lb. of uncooked beef stew meat, cut in 1-inch pieces
- 4 carrots, peeled, diced
- 4 stalks celery, diced
- 1 onion, peeled, chopped
- 1 tsp. of dried oregano
- ½ tsp. of kosher salt
- ¼ tsp. of pepper
- 2 tbsp. of tomato paste
- 1 can (14.5 oz.) of diced tomatoes
- 6 cups of beef broth
- 1 cup of pearl barley

Cooking Instructions:

1. Select the sear/sauté button and set to high. Select the start/stop to begin. Allow to preheat for about 5 minutes.

2. After 5 minutes, add oil, then add beef in batches, browning it on all sides. Remove beef and set aside. Add carrots, celery, onion, oregano, salt, and pepper to pot.

3. Cook for about 5 minutes. Add tomato paste, diced tomatoes, broth, and barley to pot and stir to combine.

4. Place browned beef back in the pot and select start/stop to turn off sear/sauté. Assemble pressure lid, make sure the pressure release valve is in the seal position.

5. Select pressure and set to high. Set time to 22 minutes. Select start/stop to begin. When pressure cooking is done, allow pressure to naturally release for 10 minutes.

6. After 10 minutes, quick release any remaining pressure by moving the pressure release valve to the vent position.

7. Carefully remove lid when unit has finished releasing pressure. When cooking is complete, soup is ready to serve.

Beef & Broccoli

Preparation time: 15 minutes

Cooking time: 20 minutes

Overall time: 35 minutes

Serves: 2 to 4 people

Recipe Ingredients:

- ½ cup of reduced-sodium soy sauce
- ½ cup of beef broth
- 3 tbsp. of cooking sherry
- 2 tbsp. of brown sugar
- 1 tbsp. of fresh ginger, peeled, minced
- ¼ tsp. of crushed red pepper
- 1 ½ lb. of uncooked flank steak, sliced against the grain into 1/2-inch thick slices
- 2/3 cup of water, divided
- 4 cups of broccoli florets
- 2 tbsp. of cornstarch
- 4 fresh scallions, chopped
- Cooked rice, for serving

Cooking Instructions:

1. In a medium bowl, combine soy sauce, broth, sherry, brown sugar, ginger, and crushed red pepper.

2. Add steak to mixture and marinate for about 15 minutes. In the meantime, place 1/2 cup water and cook and crisp basket in pot.

3. Place broccoli in basket. Assemble pressure lid, making sure the pressure release valve is in the vent position.

4. Select steam and set time to 4 minutes. Select start/stop to begin. When cooking is complete, carefully remove pressure lid.

5. Remove basket with broccoli from pot and set aside. Pour water out of pot. Add steak and marinade to pot.

6. Assemble pressure lid, making sure the pressure release valve is in the seal position. Select pressure and set to high, set time to 12 minutes.

7. Select the start/stop button to begin. When pressure cooking is complete, quick release the pressure by moving the pressure release valve to the vent position.

Lamb Shanks with Roasted Carrots

Preparation time: 10 minutes

Cooking time: 55 minutes

Serves: 2 to 4 people

Recipe Ingredients:

- 3 tbsp. of olive oil, divided
- 4 lamb shanks (about 3 lb. total)
- 2 tsp. of kosher salt, plus more for seasoning
- 2 tsp. of paprika
- 1 tsp. of ground cumin
- 1 tsp. of ground cinnamon
- 1 tsp. of ground black pepper
- 1 cup of red wine
- 2 cloves of garlic, peeled
- 1 lb. of baby carrots
- 1 tbsp. of instant flour

Cooking Instructions:

1. Add 2 tablespoons olive oil to the pot. Select sear/sauté function and set to high. Select start/stop to begin. Allow to preheat for about 5 minutes.

2. After 5 minutes, add lamb shanks to pot. Sear until browned on all sides, for about 10 minutes.

3. Add salt and spices to the pot and cook until aromatic, stirring, about one minute. Add the red wine and garlic to the pot.

4. Scrape the bottom for any browned bits. Assemble pressure lid, making sure the pressure release valve is in the seal position. Select pressure and set to high.

5. Set time to 15 minutes. Select start/stop to begin. When pressure cooking is complete, quick release the pressure by moving the valve to the vent position.

6. Carefully remove lid when unit has finished releasing pressure. Place the reversible rack in the pot over shanks, making sure rack is in the higher position.

7. Place carrots on rack. Assemble pressure lid, making sure the pressure release valve is in the seal position.

8. Select pressure and set to high. Set time to 10 minutes. Select start/stop to begin. When pressure cooking is complete, quick release the pressure by moving the pressure release valve to the vent position.

9. Carefully remove lid when unit has finished releasing pressure. Drizzle 1 tablespoon olive oil over the carrots.

10. Season the carrots with a pinch of salt, then close the crisping lid. Select broil and set time to 10 minutes. Select the start/stop button to begin.

11. When cooking is complete, remove carrots and lamb shanks from the pot and allow to rest. Select sear/sauté and set to high. Select start/stop to begin.

12. Add instant flour to the liquid in the pot, whisking constantly. Bring mixture to a boil. Once boiling, press the power button to turn off sear/sauté.

13. Ladle the sauce over the lamb and serve.

Holiday Brisket

Preparation time: 15 minutes

Cooking time: 2 hours

Overall time: 2 hours 15 minutes

Serves: 6 to 8 people

Recipe Ingredients:

- 1 tsp. of kosher salt
- 1 tsp. of garlic powder
- ½ tsp. of butcher-grind black pepper
- 2 tbsp. of olive oil, divided
- 5 lb. of brisket, excess fat trimmed, cut in half
- 2 red onions, peeled, cut into rings
- 1 cup of dried porcini mushrooms
- 1 can (18.5 ounces) of French onion soup
- 1 can (14 ounces) of stewed cherry tomatoes
- ¼ cup of sundried tomatoes, sliced
- 1 cup of red wine
- 1 large bunch fresh thyme (about 20 small stems), plus more for garnish
- 4 large carrots, peeled, cut into chunks
- ¼ cup of fresh parsley, chopped, for garnish

Cooking Instructions:

1. Select sear/sauté function and set to high mode. Select the start/stop button to begin. Allow to preheat for about 5 minutes. Stir together salt, garlic, and pepper.

2. Brush meat with 1 teaspoon of olive oil and season both sides generously with the spice mixture.

3. Add remaining oil to the pot and sear each piece of brisket, one at a time, on both sides, about 2 minutes per side. Set seared meat aside on a clean plate.

4. Press the start/stop button to turn off sear/sauté. Add onions and mushrooms to the pot.

5. Place seared brisket on top and add onion soup, stewed tomatoes, sundried tomatoes, wine, thyme, and carrots. Stir gently to combine.

6. Assemble pressure lid, making sure the pressure release valve is in the seal position. Select pressure and set to high. Set time to 1 hour and 20 minutes.

7. Select start/stop to begin. When pressure cooking is complete, quick release pressure by moving the pressure release valve to the vent position.

8. Carefully remove lid when unit has finished releasing pressure. The meat should be fork tender, so can easily insert a fork, but the meat is not falling apart.

9. Allow the meat to rest in the cooking liquid for about 30 minutes, then skim the excess fat from the top.

10. Discard the fat and remove the cooked brisket from the cooking liquid; set on clean plate.

11. Insert the reversible rack into the pot, making sure rack is in the higher position. Place brisket on the rack. Close crisping lid.

12. Select the air crisp function and set temperature to 400°F, and set time to 15 minutes. Select the start/stop button to begin.

13. When cooking is complete, remove the reversible rack with brisket. Set on a heat-proof surface and allow to rest at room temperature, tented with foil.

14. While the meat rests, select sear/sauté and set to high. With lid off, simmer liquid for about 20 to 30 minutes, or until liquid is reduced by half.

15. Just before serving, slice the brisket into 1/4-inch slices, against the grain. Pour hot juices over the brisket.

16. Serve with the sauce and vegetables, garnished with thyme and parsley, if desired.

Corned Beef & Cabbage

Preparation time: 25 minutes

Cooking time: 1 hour 18 minutes

Overall time: 1 hour 45 minutes

Serves: 6 to 8 people

Recipe Ingredients:

- 5 lb. of corned beef brisket
- 2 cups of chicken stock
- 2 cups of Irish extra stout beer
- 1 yellow onion, peeled, chopped
- 7 cloves of garlic, peeled
- 7 sprigs of fresh thyme
- 3 bay leaves
- 1 ½ lb. red or gold baby potatoes
- 1 lb. of carrots, peeled, cut in 2-inch pieces (or baby carrots)
- 1 head of green cabbage, cut in wedges
- Whole grain mustard, for serving

Cooking Instructions:

1. Place brisket in the pot, fat-side down. Add seasoning packet, stock, beer, onion, garlic, thyme, and bay leaves.

2. Assemble the pressure lid, making sure the pressure release valve is in the seal position. Select pressure and set to high mode.

3. Set time to 1 hour 15 minutes. Select the start/stop button to begin. When pressure cooking is complete, allow pressure to naturally release for about 10 minutes.

4. After 10 minutes, quick release remaining pressure by moving the pressure release valve to the vent position.

5. Carefully remove lid when unit has finished releasing pressure. Transfer brisket to a plate and tent with foil.

6. Using a wire mesh strainer, remove the herbs, onions, and aromatics from the liquid. Place potatoes, carrots, and cabbage into the pot with the liquid.

7. Assemble the pressure lid, making sure the pressure release valve is in the seal position. Select pressure and set to high mode and time to 3 minutes.

8. Select the start/stop button to begin. When pressure cooking is complete, quick release the pressure by moving the pressure release valve to the vent position.

9. Carefully remove lid when unit has finished releasing pressure. Slice brisket across the grain. Top with whole grain mustard and serve with vegetables.

SOUP AND STEW RECIPES

Quick Chicken & Rice Soup

Preparation time: 20 minutes

Cooking time: 7 minutes

Overall time: 27 people

Serves: 6 to 8 people

Recipe Ingredients:

- 6 large carrots, peeled, sliced
- 6 stalks of celery, trimmed, sliced
- 3 leeks, trimmed, cut in half lengthwise, thinly sliced
- ¾ cup of long grain white rice
- 4 sprigs of fresh thyme
- 6 cups of chicken broth, divided
- 2 lb. of boneless, skinless chicken thighs, trimmed, cut in bite-size pieces
- 2 tsp. of kosher salt, plus more for seasoning
- 2 tsp. of ground black pepper, plus more for seasoning
- 1 cup of water, plus more as needed

Cooking Instructions:

1. Place carrots, celery, leeks, rice, thyme, and 1 ½ cups of broth into the pot. Place chicken on top of vegetables and season with salt and pepper.

2. Assemble pressure lid, making sure the pressure release valve is in the seal position. Select pressure and set to high mode and set time to 2 minutes.

3. Select the start/stop button to begin. When pressure cooking is complete, allow pressure to naturally release for about 10 minutes.

4. After 10 minutes, quick release remaining pressure by moving the pressure release valve to the vent position.

5. Carefully remove lid when unit has finished releasing pressure. Remove thyme sprigs from pot.

6. Select the sear/sauté function and set to high mode. Add water and remaining 4 ½ cups of broth and let simmer for about 5 minutes to heat through.

7. Season with salt and pepper to taste. Add additional water as needed to achieve desired consistency. When cooking is complete, serve immediately.

Pot Roast Soup

Preparation time: 10 minutes

Cooking time: 35 minutes

Overall time: 45 minutes

Serves: 3 to 5 people

Recipe Ingredients:

- 2 tablespoons of avocado oil
- 1 onion diced
- 2 celery stalks diced
- 3 carrots peeled and diced
- 3 garlic of cloves minced
- ¾ cup of red wine
- 1 cup of green beans
- ½ teaspoon of fresh rosemary
- 1 (14 ounces) can of fire roasted tomatoes
- 4 cups of beef broth
- 3 cups of beef cooked
- 1 teaspoon of salt
- 1 teaspoon of pepper
- 2 teaspoons of oregano
- 1 tablespoon of gluten free flour or regular flour

Cooking Instructions:

1. Turn on the sauté feature and add the avocado oil. Add the onions, carrots, and celery and sauté until the vegetables have softened up.

2. Add the garlic next, stir until fragrant, for about one minute. Add the wine. Let it simmer a bit and reduce down, for about 3 to 5 minutes.

3. Add the rest of the ingredients. Turn off the saute feature and place the pressure cooker lid on top of the cooker.

4. Turn the valve to seal, and turn on manual pressure on high mode for about 25 minutes.

5. Once it's done you can release the pressure manually. Serve immediately and Enjoy!

Chicken Vegetable Soup

Preparation time: 5 minutes

Cooking time: 5 minutes

Overall time: 10 minutes

Serves: 2 to 4 people

Recipe Ingredients:

- 2 pounds of chicken breasts, diced
- ½ onion chopped
- 1 can of lima beans or 1 cup frozen
- 1 (16 ounces) package of frozen vegetables
- 1 (28 ounces) can of crushed tomatoes
- 1 (14.5 ounces) can of tomato sauce
- 2 cups of water (or chicken broth)
- 1 tbsp. of Italian Seasoning
- Salt and pepper, to taste

Cooking Instructions:

1. Place the diced chicken at the bottom of the Ninja Foodi.

2. Combine all of the ingredients in the pot, stir to combine. Add the lid and set to sealing.

3. Set the pressure to high mode for about 5 minutes. Do a quick release or you can do the natural release when the cooking time is up.

4. Remove the lid. Stir and enjoy. Serve with parmesan cheese and your favorite rolls.

Beef Taco Soup with Hatch Chiles

Preparation time: 10 minutes

Cooking time: 4 minutes

Overall time: 14 minutes

Serves: 4 to 6 people

Recipe Ingredients:

- 1 pound of lean ground beef
- 1 packet of taco seasoning mix or gluten-free taco seasoning mix
- 1 (15 ounces) can of black beans, drained
- 1 (14.5 ounces) can of diced tomatoes
- 1 (14.5 ounces) can of beef broth
- 1 cup of corn
- 1 cup of water
- 1/3 cup of chopped hatch chiles

Cooking Instructions:

1. Brown the ground beef by sautéing on high mode.

2. Drain the meat and return to the pot. Once the meat is browned, add in the taco seasoning.

3. Add in the black beans, tomatoes, broth, corn, and water. Stir in the chiles. Set to manual high pressure for about 4 minutes.

4. Once it comes to pressure, quick release and serve with sides of your choice such as doritos, corn chips, shredded cheese, or sour cream.

Baked Potato Soup

Preparation time:

Cooking time:

Overall time:

Serves:

Recipe Ingredients:

- 2/3 cup butter
- 2/3 cup flour
- 7 cups milk
- 4 large baking potatoes, baked, cooled, peeled and cubed, about 4 cups
- 4 green onions, (including tops) chopped
- 10 to 12 strips bacon, cooked, drained, and crumbled
- 1 1/4 cups shredded mild cheddar cheese
- 1 cup (8 ounces) sour cream
- 3/4 teaspoon salt
- 1/2 teaspoon pepper
- Celery salt, (optional to be sprinkled on top of each bowl)

Cooking Instructions:

1. Bake potatoes until fork tender, cut potatoes in halves and scoop out and set aside.

2. Chop the potatoes with peels and add as many peels as you would like and discard the remainder. Turn on Ninja to sauté mode and melt butter.

3. Slowly blend in flour with a wire whisk till thoroughly blended. Gradually add milk, whisking constantly.

4. Whisk in salt and pepper, stirring constantly. When the milk mixture is very hot; stir in the potatoes. Add green onions and potato peels.

5. Add sour cream & crumpled bacon. Switch to Slow Cook for about 2 hours, stir well and Add cheese a little at a time, until it is melted and mixed in.

6. Serve with celery salt sprinkled on top of soup, and crusty French bread.

Hearty Beef Stew

Preparation time: 10 minutes

Cooking time: 7 hours

Overall time: 7 hours 10 minutes

Serves: 6 to 8 people

Recipe Ingredients:

- 2 lb. of beef for stew,
- 1 tsp. of salt,
- ½ tsp. of ground black pepper,
- ¼ cup of all-purpose flour,
- 2 tbsp. of vegetable oil,
- 1 ½ cups of beef broth,
- 4 red potatoes, cut in half,
- 2 onions, cut in quarters,
- 1 cup of baby carrots,
- 4 cloves of garlic, chopped,
- 2 sprigs of fresh thyme or 1 teaspoon dried thyme leaves, crushed,
- 1 cup of frozen peas, thawed

Cooking Instructions:

1. Season beef with salt and black pepper and coat with flour.

2. Pour oil into pot and set to sauté function on high mode and heat oil. Add beef and cook uncovered for about 10 minutes or until browned, stirring occasionally.

3. Stir broth, potatoes, onions, carrots, garlic, and thyme in pot. Set to Slow Cook on Low mode for about 7 to 9 hours.

4. Cover and cook until beef is fork-tender. Stir in peas during last 10 minutes of cooking time.

5. Serve immediately and Enjoy!

Beef Stew & Dumplings

Preparation time: 10 minutes

Cooking time: 30 minutes

Overall time: 40 minutes

Serves: 2 to 4 people

Recipe Ingredients:

- 400g of diced beef
- 2 onions diced
- 400g of carrots, sliced chunky
- 500 potatoes peeled and cubed
- 2 tablespoons of corn flour heaped spoons
- 1 teaspoon of mixed herbs
- 1 cup of beef stock
- Dumplings
- Pack of dumpling mix

Cooking Instructions:

1. Add the onions and diced beef to pot and click Sear/Sauté on high mode and press the start button.

2. Cook until beef is no longer red on the outside, do not brown. Stir occasionally Add in the potatoes and carrots and stir through.

3. Add in the 2 heaped spoons of corn flour, mixed herbs and a little salt and pepper. Stir through until you can no longer see dry flour.

4. Pour in the stock, do not stir. Put the pressure lid on and pressure cook on high for about 15 minutes.

5. When done leave for about 5 minutes then vent. Stir through thoroughly then add in the made-up dumplings.

6. Bake/Roast for about 15 minutes at 180°c. allow to cool before serving.

Beef Stew

Preparation time: 5 minutes

Cooking time: 35 minutes

Overall time: 40 minutes

Serves: 3 to 5 people

Recipe Ingredients:

- 1 ½ pounds of stew meat, cubed
- 1 tablespoon of olive oil
- 1 teaspoon of salt
- 1 teaspoon of pepper
- 1 teaspoon of Italian seasoning
- 2 tablespoons of Worcestershire sauce
- 3 cloves of garlic, minced
- 1 onion, diced
- 1 bag baby carrots
- 1 pound of potato, diced
- 2 ½ cup of beef broth
- 10 ounces of tomato sauce
- 2 tablespoons of cornstarch
- 2 tablespoons of water

Cooking Instructions:

1. Dice your onions, chop the potatoes into 1-inch cubes and mince your garlic. Set your Ninja Foodi on sauté, high and allow it warm up.

2. Add the oil now too, use olive oil or vegetable oil. Add the stew meat, salt, pepper, and Italian seasoning to the Ninja Foodi. You want to brown the meat on all sides.

3. Once the meat is browned, add the beef stock and use a spatula or wooden spoon to clean off the sides of the pot.

4. add the Worcestershire sauce, garlic, onion, carrots, potatoes, and tomato sauce. Place the pressure-cooking lid on your Ninja Foodi.

5. Ensure the steam vent is closed. Set the Ninja Foodi on pressure cook, high for about 35 minutes.

6. When it's done, let it do a natural release for about 10 minutes then open the steam valve and finish with a quick release.

7. In a small bowl, combine the cornstarch and water. Stir the mixture until the cornstarch is dissolved.

8. Pour the mixture into the beef stew and stir until the sauce starts to thicken. This is great with a piece of crusty bread too.

Chicken and Wild Rice Soup

Preparation time: 5 minutes

Cooking time: 30 minutes

Overall time: 35 minutes

Serves: 2 to 4 people

Recipe Ingredients:

- 5 pounds of chicken, whole could substitute other chicke pieces.
- 1⅓ cups of wild rice
- 2⅔ cups of chicken stock
- 8 cups of water this will vary based on chicken size, etc.
- 1 cup of onion, chopped
- 1 cup of celery, chopped
- 1 cup of carrots, chopped
- 1 cup of mushrooms
- 2 tablespoons of olive oil can substitute grape seed or other oil.
- 2 tablespoons of chicken bouillon granules
- ¾ tsp ground white pepper
- ½ teaspoon of salt
- ½ cup of butter
- 3 cups of milk
- 1 cup of half and half cream
- ¾ cup of white wine
- ¾ cup of flour

Cooking Instructions:

1. Place the wild rice and prepared bouillon in the Ninja Foodi. Pressure cook on High for about 15 minutes.

2. Quickly release pressure when the cooking time is up. Drain the excess liquid from the rice and set the rice aside.

3. Sauté vegies and set the Ninja Foodi to Sauté and add oil. Sauté the onions, until soft and translucent.

4. Add carrots, celery and mushrooms. Sauté for about another minute and turn off the Sauté function. Add the chicken to the Ninja Foodi.

5. Add enough water to reach the 10 to 12 cup line. Larger chickens go to 12 cups, smaller go to the 10 cup line.

6. Pressure cook on High mode for about 20 minutes. Quick Release the pressure. Remove the chicken to cool and shred.

7. Turn the Sauté function back on and add the rice back to the pot. Add the bouillon granules, white pepper and salt.

8. Simmer for about 15 minutes. If you need to add more water do so at this time. While the soup is simmering, in a medium saucepan melt butter on medium heat.

9. Butter and flour Whisk in the flour until smooth. Smooth flour Slowly whisk in the milk and half and half. Continue cooking until bubbly and thick.

10. Whisk in milk to keep the milk mixture from curdling or clumping, you cannot just add to the simmering pot quickly.

11. Instead add about ¾ to 1 cup of the broth mixture to the milk mixture in the saucepan stirring well.

12. Add the milk mixture to the Ninja Foodi and mix well. Add the shredded chicken and white wine. Heat through for about 10-15 minutes.

13. Serve immediately and Enjoy!

Beef Taco Soup with Hatch Chiles

Preparation time: 10 minutes

Cooking time: 4 minutes

Overall time: 14 minutes

Serves: 4 to people

Recipe Ingredients:

- 1 pound of lean ground beef
- 1 packet of taco seasoning mix or gluten-free taco seasoning mix
- 1 (15 ounces) can of black beans, drained
- 1 (14.5 ounces) can of diced tomatoes
- 1 (14.5 ounces) can of beef broth
- 1 cup of corn
- 1 cup of water
- 1/3 cup of chopped hatch chiles or canned chiles

Cooking Instructions:

1. Brown the ground beef by sautéing on high mode. Drain the meat and return to the pot.

2. Once the meat is browned, add in the taco seasoning and add in the black beans, tomatoes, broth, corn, and water, stir in the chiles.

3. Set to manual high pressure for about 4 minutes. Once it comes to pressure, quick release.

4. Serve with sides of your choice such as doritos, corn chips, shredded cheese, or sour cream.

Chicken Noodle Soup

Preparation time:

Cooking time:

Overall time: 1 hour

Serves:

Recipe Ingredients:

- Chicken
- 48 ounces of chicken broth
- Thyme (dried or fresh)
- Cracked pepper
- Salt
- 1 Onion
- 1 pound of carrot chips
- 1 bunch of celery
- 1 tablespoon of minced garlic
- ½ cup of broth base & seasoning
- 12 cups of water
- 1 pound of egg noodles

Cooking Instructions:

1. With the basket inserted into the Nano-ceramic liner, add chicken, 48 ounces of chicken broth, and sprinkle chicken generously with thyme.

2. Add a dash of cracked pepper and salt also. Put on pressure cooker lid and set valve to seal position.

3. Set to pressure cook on high mode for about 20 minutes. Press start. Cut up onions and celery.

4. Whisk broth base and some of the water. When Foodi timer is done, quickly release pressure. Carefully remove basket and set in sink, let chicken set to cool.

5. To the broth left in the Nano ceramic liner, add onions, celery, carrots, garlic, water broth base mix, the rest of the water, and sprinkle more thyme and pepper.

6. Add pressure cooker lid on high mode. Set timer to 5 minutes. Once chicken has cooled to the touch, remove and discard bones and skin.

7. When timer goes off for the Foodi, quick release. Add separated chicken meat. Top with noodles but don't stir them in. Just allow the noodles to lay on top.

8. Add pressure cooker lid on high mode, and cook for 5 minutes. When timer goes off, let natural release 5 minutes. Quick release, stir, and enjoy.

Beef Taco Soup with Hatch Chiles

Preparation time: 10 minutes

Cooking time: 4 minutes

Overall time: 14 minutes

Serves: 4 to 6 people

Recipe Ingredients:

- 1 pound of lean ground beef
- 1 packet of taco seasoning mix or gluten-free taco seasoning mix
- 1 (15 ounces) can of black beans, drained
- 1 (14.5 ounces) can of diced tomatoes
- 1 (14.5 ounces) can of beef broth
- 1 cup of corn
- 1 cup of water
- 1/3 cup of chopped hatch chiles or canned chiles

Cooking Instructions:

1. Begin by browning the ground beef by sautéing on high mode. Drain the meat and return to the pot.

2. Once the meat is browned, add in the taco seasoning and add in the black beans, tomatoes, broth, corn, and water.

3. Stir in the chiles and set to manual high pressure for about 4 minutes. Once it comes to pressure, do a quick pressure release.

4. Serve with sides of your choice such as doritos, corn chips, shredded cheese, or sour cream.

Sausage & Spinach Tortellini Soup

Preparation time: 5 minutes

Cooking time: 10 minutes

Overall time: 30 minutes

Serves: 4 to 6 people

Recipe Ingredients:

- 1 lb. of ground pork sausage
- 1 onion chopped- about 2 cups
- 2 carrots chopped- about 1 cup
- 1 tbsp. of minced garlic
- 1 tbsp. of Italian seasoning
- ½ tsp. of salt
- ½ tsp. of pepper
- 2 (14.5 ounces) cans of beef broth
- ¼ cup of cornstarch
- ¼ cup of water
- 1 (10 ounces) package of frozen spinach or 2.5 cups fresh
- 12 ounces of frozen tortellini
- 1 cup of milk
- 3 (12 oz.) cans of evaporated milk

Cooking Instructions:

1. Turn on your Ninja Foodi on the sauté function.

2. Add sausage and garlic, cook until the sausage is browned evenly. Add carrots and onion.

3. Cook until the onion is translucent for about 4 minutes Turn off Ninja Foodi Add salt, pepper, Italian seasoning, beef stock and tortellini.

4. Put the pressure cooker lid on the Ninja Foodi Cook on High Pressure for about 3 minutes, ensure the valve is on sealing position.

5. When the time is up, move seal to vent to quick release pressure Turn Ninja Foodi off and then back on to the sauté function.

6. Add in evaporated milk, add milk and sauté until boiling Mix cornstarch and water in mason jar

7. Shake and add cornstarch and water mixture Stir Add the spinach and cook until thickened, for about 3 minutes.

8. Serve immediately and Enjoy!

Chicken Soup

Preparation time: 5 minutes

Cooking time: 25 minutes

Overall time: 30 minutes

Serves: 2 to 4 people

Recipe Ingredients:

- 6 carrots, sliced
- 6 stalks of celery, sliced
- 1 medium onion, thinly chopped
- 2 garlic cloves, minced
- 1 ½ lb. of boneless, skinless chicken thighs, cut up into bite size pieces
- 1 cup of orzo pasta
- 6 cups of chicken or bone broth
- 2 dried bay leaves
- 2 tsp. of salt
- More salt & pepper to taste

Cooking Instructions:

1. Add the prepared carrots, celery, onion, garlic, orzo, bay leaves to the cooking pot of the Ninja Foodi.

2. Cut up chicken to bite size pieces and add to the top of the vegetables. Sprinkle with 2 teaspoons of salt and add 1 ½ cups of chicken or bone broth.

3. Install the pressure lid, make sure to set the release valve to the seal position. Choose the pressure function and set to high.

4. Set the time to 2 minutes and press the start button to begin. The pressure takes about 10 minutes to build.

5. When the pressure cooking is complete, allow the pressure to naturally release for 10 minutes.

6. After the 10 minutes, quick release any remaining pressure by switching the vent release valve to vent.

7. And then carefully remove the lid and remove the bay leaves and discard. Set the Ninja Foodi to sear/sauté and turn the temp to high.

8. Add remaining broth and simmer for just 5 minutes until heated through. Use fresh herbs as a garnish if you'd like, but it is totally optional.

Split Pea Soup

Preparation time: 5 minutes

Cooking time: 15 minutes

Overall time 30 minutes

Serves: 8 to 10 people

Recipe Ingredients:

- 3 cups of diced ham
- 1 ham bone
- 1 pound of split peas
- 2 ribs of celery, diced
- 2 carrots, sliced
- 1 small onion, diced (or half a large onion)
- 3 strips of bacon
- 1 large bay leaf or a few small ones
- 8 cups of chicken broth
- Pepper, to taste
- 1 tsp. of garlic powder
- 1 tablespoon of oil
- Sour cream for garnish

Cooking Instructions:

1. Press sauté on the Foodi. If using the bacon, begin to sauté now to render some of the fat into the pot.

2. Add the 1 tablespoon of oil to the pot to heat. When the bacon is rendered, add the celery and onion to sauté in the fat.

3. If not using the bacon, simply add the celery, onions, and carrots to saute. Saute the veggies for about 3 minutes.

4. Add the ham and spices and continue to sauté another minute. Add the ham bone (or ham hock) and peas.

5. Add the broth and place the lid on the pot and turn the toggle switch to "seal". Press manual to "high' and set the time for about 15 minutes.

6. After the cook time is up, do a natural release for about 10 minutes. Then slowly release the remaining pressure in the pot.

7. Upon opening the lid, give the soup a good stir as a lot of the peas may be settled on the bottom.

8. Carefully, remove the bone from the soup, and take any remaining ham off the bone.

9. Add the ham back to the pot and give it another stir. Remove the bay leaf, upon serving.

10. Drizzle some sour cream on top for a pretty presentation and to add a bit more richness to the soup.

FISH AND SEAFOOD RECIPES

Miso Glazed Salmon with Bok Choy

Preparation time: 10 minutes

Cooking time: 10 minutes

Overall time: 20 minutes

Serves: 2 to 4 people

Recipe Ingredients:

- 1 cup of jasmine rice, rinsed
- ¾ cup of water
- 4 frozen skinless salmon fillets (4 ounces, 1-inch thick each)
- 1 tsp. of kosher salt
- 2 tbsp. of red miso paste
- 2 tbsp. of butter, softened
- 2 heads of baby bok choy, stems on, rinsed, cut in half
- ¼ cup of mirin
- 1 tsp. of sesame oil
- Sesame seeds, for garnish

Cooking Instructions:

1. Place rice and water into the pot. Stir to combine. Place reversible rack in pot, making sure rack is in the higher position.

2. Season salmon with salt, then place on rack. Assemble pressure lid, making sure the pressure release valve is in the seal position.

3. Select pressure and set to high and set time to 2 minutes. Select start/stop to begin. While salmon and rice are cooking, stir together miso and butter to form a paste.

4. Toss bok choy with mirin and sesame oil. When pressure cooking is done, quick release the pressure by moving the pressure release valve to the vent position.

5. Carefully remove lid when unit has finished releasing pressure. Gently pat salmon dry with paper towel, then spread miso butter evenly on top of the fillets.

6. Add bok choy to the rack. Close crisping lid. Select broil and set time to 7 minutes. Select start/stop to begin, checking for doneness after 5 minutes.

7. When cooking is complete, remove salmon from rack and serve with bok choy and rice. Garnish with sesame seeds, if desired.

Shrimp & Grits

Preparation time: 10 minutes

Cooking time: 15 minutes

Overall time: 25 minutes

Serves: 2 to 4 people

Recipe Ingredients:

- 3 cups of water, divided
- 1 cup of grits (or coarse grind cornmeal)
- 3 tsp. of kosher salt, divided
- 16 frozen uncooked jumbo shrimp, peeled, deveined, patted dry
- Juice of 1 lemon
- 1 tsp. of olive oil
- 2 cloves of garlic, peeled, minced
- 1 tsp. of chili powder
- 1 tsp. of garlic powder
- 1 tsp. of black pepper
- ¼ cup of butter, cut in 8 pieces
- ¼ cup of grated Parmesan cheese
- 2 tbsp. of fresh parsley, chopped, for garnish
- 2 scallions, thinly sliced, for garnish

Cooking Instructions:

1. Pour ½ cup of water into the pot. Place grits, 2 teaspoons of salt, and remaining 2 ½ cups of water into the ninja, stir to combine.

2. Place pan onto the reversible rack, making sure rack is in the lower position. Place rack with pan in pot.

3. Assemble pressure lid, making sure the pressure release valve is in the seal position.

4. Select pressure and set to high mode and set time to 4 minutes. Select the start/stop button to begin.

5. While grits are cooking, place shrimp in a medium bowl and toss them with lemon juice, olive oil, garlic, chili powder, garlic powder, pepper, and remaining salt.

6. Coat thoroughly and set it aside. When pressure cooking is complete, allow pressure to natural release for about 10 minutes.

7. After 10 minutes, quick release remaining pressure by moving the pressure release valve to the vent position.

8. Carefully remove lid when unit has finished releasing pressure. Stir the butter and cheese into the grits until completely melted.

9. Lay shrimp on top of grits and close crisping lid. Select bake/roast, set temperature to 375°F, and set time to 10 minutes.

10. Select the start/stop button to begin. When cooking is complete, garnish with parsley and scallions and serve.

Garlic Shrimp with Risotto Primavera

Preparation time: 15 minutes

Cooking time: 25 minutes

Overall time: 40 minutes

Serves: 4 to 5 people

Recipe Ingredients:

- 2 tbsp. of olive oil, divided
- 1 small onion, peeled, finely diced
- 4 cloves of garlic, peeled, minced, divided
- 3 tsp. of kosher salt, divided
- 5 ½ cups of chicken or vegetable stock
- 2 cups of Arborio rice
- 16 uncooked jumbo shrimp (fresh or defrosted), peeled, deveined
- 2 tsp. of garlic powder
- 1 tsp. of ground black pepper
- ½ tsp. of crushed red pepper (optional)
- 2 tbsp. of butter
- Juice of 1 lemon
- 1 bunch of asparagus, trimmed, cut in 1-inch pieces
- 1 ½ cups of grated Parmesan cheese, plus more for serving

Cooking Instructions:

1. Select sear/sauté function and set to mid high mode. Select the start/stop button to begin, allow to preheat for about 5 minutes.

2. Add 1 tablespoon oil and onion to pot. Sauté until softened, for about 5 minutes and add half the garlic.

3. Cook until fragrant, about 1 minute. Season with 2 teaspoons salt. Add stock and rice to pot.

4. Assemble pressure lid, making sure the pressure release valve is in the seal position.

5. Select pressure and set to high mode and set time to 7 minutes. Select the start/stop button to begin.

6. While rice is cooking, toss shrimp in the remaining oil, garlic, salt, garlic powder, black pepper, and crushed red pepper in a mixing bowl.

7. When pressure cooking is complete, allow pressure to natural release for about 10 minutes.

8. After 10 minutes, quick release remaining pressure by moving the pressure release valve to the vent position.

9. Carefully remove lid when unit has finished releasing pressure. Stir butter, lemon juice, and asparagus into the rice until evenly incorporated.

10. Place reversible rack inside pot over risotto, making sure rack is in the higher position. Place shrimp on rack.

11. Close crisping lid and select broil and set time to 8 minutes. Select start/stop to begin. When cooking is complete, remove rack from pot.

12. Stir parmesan into the risotto. Top with shrimp and parmesan and serve immediately.

Shrimp Scampi Linguini

Preparation time: 5 minutes

Cooking time: 15 minutes

Overall time: 20 minutes

Serves: 6 to 8 people

Recipe Ingredients:

- 1 lb. of linguini
- 1 lb. of 31/40 shrimp
- Salt and pepper (to taste)
- 3 tbsp. of olive oil
- 3 tbsp. of butter (salted)
- 2 tbsp. of garlic (minced)
- 1 cup of dry white wine
- 1 cup of chicken broth
- ¼ tsp. Of red pepper flakes
- 1 lemon (juice of the lemon)
- ¼ cup of parmesan cheese (shredded)

Cooking Instructions:

1. Turn Ninja Foodi on sauté on high mode. Pour in olive oil. Add butter and stir. Add shrimp, season with salt and pepper and then stir.

2. Add garlic and juice of one lemon. Be careful not to get the lemon seeds in the pot. Pour in white wine and chicken broth.

3. Add red pepper flakes and stir. Break linguine in half and add in layers, criss crossing each layer so the pasta does not stick to itself.

4. Once all pasta has been added to the pot, press pasta into liquid as much as possible, without stirring.

5. Once you have added the pasta. If you do, your pasta may burn to the bottom of the pan. Put pressure cooker lid on Ninja Foodi and move valve to "seal" position.

6. Change Ninja Foodi to "pressure cook" setting on high mode for about 3 minutes and push start.

7. When timer beeps, quick release pressure by moving valve to vent position. Turn Ninja Foodi off.

8. Open Ninja Foodi lid and stir shrimp and pasta until its well combined. Don't panic if your pasta is not 100% cooked.

9. It will continue to cook after you add in the parmesan cheese. Add parmesan cheese and stir.

10. Close the Ninja Foodi lid and let the pasta and sauce continue to combine for about 5 minutes. Stir and Enjoy!

Lobster Tails

Preparation time: 5 minutes

Cooking time: 5 minutes

Overall time: 10 minutes

Serves: 4 to 6 people

Recipe Ingredients:

- 4 (4 to 6 oz.) of lobster tails
- 1 cup Liquid, use water, chicken broth, vegetable broth or seafood broth.

Cooking Instructions:

1. Cut the shell of the lobster down the back with kitchen shears, from the top to the bottom.

2. Do not cut through the end of the tail, stop cutting when you get to the last section of the tail. Separate the meat from the shell by pulling the shell apart.

3. Do not fully operate the shell as you want to be able to lay the semi-connected lobster meat on top of the shell for cooking and presentation.

4. Leave the last 20% of the lobster meat connected to the shell. After pulling the lobster meat away from the shell, gently close lobster shell under the meat.

5. Lay the meat on top of the shell. It's okay if small pieces of the shell break off during this process. Apply compound butter to butterflied lobster tails.

6. Using a tablespoon, scoop out about 1.5 tablespoons of compound butter and place on top of the butterflied lobster tails.

7. Push down a bit to make sure that the compound butter is stuck to the lobster tail pretty well.

8. Place lobster tails with compound butter on them into a steamer basket standing up and leaning against the side of the basket.

9. The trailside should be facing down and the meat side should be at the top inside of the basket.

10. Place steamer basket filled with your lobster tails in the Ninja Foodi. Pour in 1 cup of liquid- you can use water, vegetable broth, seafood stock or chicken broth.

11. Close Ninja Foodi pressure cooker lid and move valve to seal position. Pressure cook lobster tails on high mode for about 2 minutes.

12. While lobsters are cooking, microwave the remaining compound butter so that you can use it as the dipping sauce for the lobster tails.

13. Microwave in increments of 15 seconds until butter has fully melted. Stir well and pour into small dishes for serving. when timer sounds, quick release all pressure.

14. This should take about 2 minutes. Once all pressure has been released, open pressure cooker lid and remove lobsters from the Ninja Foodi.

15. Serve and eat immediately.

Bang Bang Shrimp

Preparation time: 15 minutes

Cooking time: 20 minutes

Overall time: 35 minutes

Serves: 2 to 4 people

Recipe Ingredients:

- ½ cup of all-purpose flour
- 2 large eggs
- 1 cup of fine breadcrumbs can substitute planko breadcrumbs if desired
- 2 tablespoons of grapeseed oil can substitute olive oil
- 1 teaspoon of garlic powder
- ½ teaspoon of kosher salt
- ½ teaspoon black pepper, ground
- 1 pound of uncooked large shrimp if frozen they should be thawed first
- ⅓ cup of mayonnaise
- ⅓ cup of sweet and spicy thai chili sauce
- 1 tablespoon of sriracha sauce
- 1 tablespoon lime juice
- 2 teaspoons of honey add more to taste and get to the right heat level.
- Kosher salt to taste

Cooking Instructions:

1. Using three shallow bowls set up dipping station. In the first bowl add the flour, in the second whisk the eggs.

2. In the third one mix the breadcrumbs, garlic powder, oil, salt and pepper. Coat shrimp in flour shaking off excess.

3. Dip in egg and roll in the breadcrumb mixture. Preheat the Foodi to 400°F and set time for about 5 minutes.

4. Once preheated and 5 minutes is complete, open lid and add shrimp as a single layer to the basket.

5. Switch to the Air Crisp function in Foodi that allows for a second layer. Set Air crisp temperature to 400°F for about 10 minutes. Repeat with other batches as needed.

6. While shrimp is cooking make the sauce. Whisk together the mayonoise, sweetand spicy Thai chili sauce, sriracha sauce, lime juice and honey.

7. Make sure they are well combined and then add salt to taste. When shrimp are complete drizzle some sauce over shrimp.

8. Serve the remaining sauce for dipping.

Crab Legs

Preparation time: 5 minutes

Cooking time: 5 minutes

Overall time: 10 minutes

Serves: 2 to 4 people

Recipe Ingredients:

- 4 crab leg clusters
- 2 tbsp. of garlic-minced or chopped
- 1 tbsp. of tony chachere's seasoning
- 1 cup of water
- 1 lemon-sliced

Cooking Instructions:

1. Place trivet in Ninja Foodi, pour water into pot and add garlic to pot.

2. Add Tony Chachere's seasoning, place sliced lemons on trivet and add crab legs to pot Close lid and move valve to seal position.

3. Cook on high mode for about 2 minutes. When timer beeps move seal to release and quick release all pressure.

4. Once pressure is released take off the lid. Let crab Legs continue to steam in the Ninja Foodi for up to 5 minutes

5. Serve with melted butter

Cajun Shrimp Boil

Preparation time: 10 minutes

Cook Time: 30 minutes

Overall time: 40 minutes

Serves: 4 to 6 people

Recipe Ingredients:

- 2 onions quartered, I used Vidalia
- 3 ears of corn
- 6 Yukon gold potatoes
- 1 jalapeno pepper
- 2 red chili peppers dried
- 1 bulb of garlic
- 2 cups of chicken stock
- 14 oz. of Andouille sausage
- 4 sprigs Thyme
- 1 lemon halved
- 2 pounds of shrimp large & frozen
- 1 zucchini

Whole Spice Seasoning Blend:

- 1 tablespoon of black peppercorns
- ½ tablespoon of mustard seed
- ½ tablespoon of cumin seed
- 3 bay leaves
- 2 teaspoons of coarse sea salt

Shrimp Seasoning:

- ¼ teaspoon of smoked paprika
- ¾ teaspoon of garlic powder
- ¼ teaspoon of mustard dry ground or substitute mustard seed
- ½ teaspoon of sea salt
- ¼ teaspoon of pepper

Cajun Butter:

- ½ cup of salted butter 1 stick
- 1 teaspoon of cumin ground
- 1 teaspoon of brown sugar
- ¾ teaspoon of garlic powder

- ¾ teaspoon of onion powder
- ¼ teaspoon of smoked paprika
- 1/8 teaspoon of chipotle ground

Cooking Instructions:

1. Place the quartered onions in the inner pot. Cut the ends off of 3 ears of corn and leave the husks on.

2. Place corn in the inner pot. Quarter the potatoes and place in the inner pot. Add in the whole spice seasoning blend.

3. Add 2 cups of chicken stock. Add in one bulb of garlic, peeled and smashed. Cut the Andouille sausage in 1/2 lengthwise on the diagonal and add to inner pot.

4. Add in the Thyme and lemon cut in half Pour about ½ cup of water over frozen shrimp and toss with shrimp seasoning. Add to inner pot.

5. Cut the zucchini in half and place in pot. Put the pressure lid on and turn the valve to seal.

6. Set the pressure on high mode for about 2 minutes. When the time is up immediately release the pressure and remove the lid.

7. Melt the Cajun butter and pour over shrimp boil. Serve and Enjoy!

Linguine and Shrimp

Preparation time: 10 minutes

Cooking time: 35 minutes

Overall time: 45 minutes

Serves: 4 to 6 people

Recipe Ingredients:

- 8 ounces of baby spinach leaves divided half
- 1 cup of sun-dried tomatoes rinsed and patted dry
- 6 garlic clovers
- 8 ounces of sliced mushrooms
- 1 pound of linguine (uncooked)
- 4 cups of chicken stock
- 1 cup of white cooking wine (mine had lemon in it)
- 4 ounces of parmesan cheese
- Garlic, herb, black pepper and sea salt
- Himalayan pink salt, garlic, and onion (approx 5 dashes to each step in pot recipe.
- ½ stick of butter
- 1 pound of scallops
- 2 pounds of shrimp cleaned and de veined. may use frozen

Cooking Instructions:

1. Put all the ingredients into the pot except half the spinach and parm. Pressure Cook on High mode for about 8 minutes.

2. Naturally Release for about 10 minutes, add 2 pounds of shrimp, 1 pounds of scallops and ½ stick of butter.

3. The spices used are blends, garlic herb, black pepper and sea salt. Himalayan pink salt, black pepper and garlic. Garlic onion, black pepper and sea salt.

4. Add a few shakes to each side as you tossed them in the panto get the seafood covered.

5. After the noodles were cooked, put the shrimp and scallops in the spring form pan and seasoned and added butter and cut up in chunks.

6. Place the meat rack in low position above the noodles. Air Crisp for about 12 to 14 minutes at 390ºF

7. Turn them every 5 minutes or so. You can add the rest of the parm and spinach to the noodles when complete.

8. plate the pasta and the seafood on top of noodles, and tossed some scallions and a little fresh parsley on top.   Eat and enjoy!

Grill Lemon Pepper Shrimp for a Salad

Preparation time: 5 minutes

Cooking time: 10 minutes

Overall time: 15 minutes

Serves: 2 to 4 people

Recipe Ingredients:

- Shrimp
- Vegetables oil
- Lemon pepper seasoning
- Salad

Cooking Instructions:

1. Spray shrimp with vegetable oil seasoning with lemon pepper.

2. Pre heat grill on mid high mode, cook for about 6 minutes but will only be cooking about 2 minutes per side.

3. Flip after 2 minutes of cooking keep an eye on them this doesn't take long.

Rice Low Country Red Rice with Shrimp and Scallops

Preparation time: 10 minutes

Cooking time: 35 minutes

Overall time: 45 minutes

Serves: 2 to 4 people

Recipe Ingredients

- 1 (15 oz.) can of diced tomato
- 1 ½ cups of chicken broth the amount will vary
- 1 red or yellow bell pepper
- 1 onion
- 2 garlic cloves
- 4 fully cooked smoked sausages
- 1 lb. of scallops
- 1 ½ lb. of large shrimp peeled and deveined
- 2 tsp. of seasoned salt
- 2 cups of long grain white rice

Cooking Instructions:

1. Drain the tomatoes and reserve the juices and add enough chicken broth to the tomato juice to equal 2 ¼ cups of Dice the onion, pepper and garlic

2. Cut the sausage into chunks, pat the scallops and shrimp dry and season the shrimp with seasoning salt. Heat the pressure cooker on the sear/saute function.

3. Pour in oil and brown the scallops and shrimp in batches for about 2 minutes per side.

4. Remove the shrimp and scallops and place them in the refrigerator until ready to use. Brown the sausage for about 5 minutes then add peppers and onions.

5. Sauté the sausage, peppers and onions for about 5 minutes until the vegetables are softened Add the garlic and stir for about 1 minute,

6. stir in the tomatoes and rice and pour in the tomato juice/chicken broth. Cook under high pressure for about 3 minutes then natural release for 10 minutes

7. Release remaining pressure. remove the lid then gently stir in the shrimp and scallops and serve it up

Herbed Salmon

Preparation time: 5 minutes

Cooking time: 5 minutes

Overall time: 10 minutes

Serves: 2 to 4 people

Recipe Ingredients:

- 8 ounces of sizzle fish salmon filets, i used two, 4-oz sizzle fish sockeye salmon filets
- 1 teaspoon of herbes de provence
- ¼ teaspoon of natural ancient sea salt
- ¼ teaspoon of black pepper
- ¼ teaspoon of smoked paprika
- 2 tablespoon of olive oil
- 1 tablespoon of medlee seasoned butter

Cooking Instructions:

1. Dry your filets with a paper towel and run the surface gently to ensure that there are no bones.

2. Drizzle the olive oil on the fish and rub it in on both sides of the fix Mix the seasonings & sprinkle them on both sides of the fish.

3. Turn on your Air Crisp mode on 390ºF and cook for about 5 to 8 minutes. Checking the fish, increase the time by 1 additional minutes until it flakes easily with a fork.

4. Melt the seasoned butter for about 30 seconds in the microwave and pour it over the fish before eating.

Fish and Grits

Preparation time: 10 minutes

Cooking time: 30 minutes

Overall time: 40 minutes

Serves: 1 to 3 people

Recipe Ingredients:

- 3 cups of chicken broth
- 1 cup of heavy cream
- 1 cup of stone ground grits
- 2 tablespoons of butter
- 1 teaspoon of salt
- 2 pieces of tilapia fish
- 2 teaspoons of blackened or Cajun seasoning
- Vegetable oil in a spray bottle

Cooking Instructions:

1. Place chicken broth, heavy cream, grits, salt and butter in Ninja Foodi pressure cooker insert. Stir and over with pressure cooker cover.

2. Make sure valve is set to sealing position. Cook on High Pressure for about 8 minutes.

3. Once the 8 minutes is up, allow the Ninja Foodi to natural release for 10 minutes. Press cancel and release the remaining pressure by turning the valve to Vent.

4. Meanwhile, season fish with blackened or Cajun seasoning by first spraying the fish, then rubbing the seasoning into both sides of the fish.

5. Once all pressure is released, open foodi and stir grits. Place a piece of heavy duty foil on top of the grits to cover. Lay the seasoned fish on top of the foil.

6. Spray again with oil. Close the Air Crisp lid on the ninja foodi. Cook at 400°F for about 10 minutes or until fish can be easily flaked with a fork.

7. Serve fish over grits and Enjoy

Ninja Salmon

Preparation time: 5 minutes

Cooking time: 4 minutes

Overall time: 9 minutes

Serves: 2 to 4 people

Recipe Ingredients:

- 2 salmon fillets
- 1 cup of water
- Juice from 1 lemon, about ½ cup
- Lemon slices
- 5 sprigs of fresh dill (or rosemary)
- Salt and pepper to taste

Cooking Instructions:

1. Pour water and lemon juice into the Ninja Foodi. Add lemon slices and dill. Add the wire rack/trivet into the pot at the lowest setting.

2. Add the fillets to the rack/trivet, cut to fit if needed. Add the lemon slices on top of the salmon.

3. Sprinkle with salt and pepper. Secure the pressure cooker lid that comes with the Ninja Foodi.

4. Make sure the valve is set to seal, use the manual settings and cook on high pressure for about 4 minutes.

5. Add an additional minute if the fillet is frozen. Once done, release the valve to vent (quick release) and then open the lid.

6. Serve the salmon immediately or store in fridge.

Lobster Tails

Preparation time: 5 minutes

Cooking time: 5 minutes

Overall time: 10 minutes

Serves: 2 to 4 people

Recipe Ingredients

- 2 lobster tails (mine were about 1/2 lb./tail)
- ½ tsp. of salt
- ½ tsp. of pepper
- 1 cup of water
- 1 tbsp. of butter
- Pinch of garlic powder
- 2 tbsp. of butter, melted
- 1 tsp. of paprika
- Melted butter, for dipping (optional)

Cooking Instructions:

1. With a sharp, clean kitchen shears, cut the shell of the lobster tail right down the middle.

2. With both hands, pry the shell apart, loosening the meat of the lobster from the bottom, sides and top of the shell.

3. Once the meat is loosened, carefully pull the meat through the top of the shell and place it on top of the opened shell. Season lobster meat with salt and pepper.

4. Add water and one tablespoon of butter to cooking pot. Place Foodi rack in lower position in the pot and position lobster tails on rack.

5. Put pressure cooking lid on foodi and make sure pressure release valve is in the seal position. Select high pressure for about 2 minutes.

6. Quickly release pressure and combine garlic powder and melted butter. Brush tails with garlic butter mixture.

7. Sprinkle tails with paprika. Air crisp at 375°F for about 2 minutes, brushing tails again with garlic butter halfway through cook time.

8. Remove tails from Foodi and enjoy with melted butter.

SNACK AND APPETIZER RECIPES
Ninja Popcorn
Preparation time: 5 minutes

Cooking time: 10 minutes

Overall time: 15 minutes

Serves: 5 to 7 people

Recipe Ingredients:

- 3 tablespoons of oil whatever kind you like
- ½ cup of popcorn kernels
- ½ teaspoon of salt
- 4 tablespoons of butter salted and room temp

Cooking Instructions:

1. Measure out a piece of foil that is 4" larger than the diameter of the inner pot and wide enough to be able to fold into a pouch.

2. Tuck the ends under the lip of the inner pot and make multiple holes with a thin sharp object.

3. Add the 3 tablespoons of oil to the inner pot and 1 un-popped corn kernel. Turn the Ninja Foodi on High Sear/Sauté function and cover with a silicone or glass lid.

4. While you are waiting for the one kernel to pop, cut or spread your butter on the foil.

5. When you hear the kernel pop, add in the remaining un-popped kernels and the salt. Stir to combine.

6. Close up the foil packet and secure by tucking under the lip of the inner pot. Cover with silicone cover or glass lid.

7. Leave the sear/sauté on high until to begin to hear the kernels rapidly popping, turn the heat down to medium/low.

8. Insert a spatula or wooden spoon and stir the bottom to move the kernels around. Once the popping has slowed down to about 1 pop every few seconds.

9. Turn the Ninja Foodi off and stir again. If there is any butter left in the foil, shake it over the popcorn and stir. Serve and enjoy!

Kale Chips

Preparation time 10 minutes

Cooking time: 4 minutes

Overall time 15 minutes

Serves: 4 to 6 people

Recipe Ingredients:

- 1 bunch of kale curly kale is best, washed, dried, remove stems
- 2 tablespoon of olive oil
- ¼ teaspoon of seasoned salt or 1/2 tsp. dry ranch dressing mix

Cooking Instructions:

1. Wash your kale and set out on countertop on paper towels to completely dry. Remove middle stems and cut leaves into large bite size pieces, they will shrink.

2. Put pieces into a bowl and drizzle olive oil on, sprinkle on seasoned salt or ranch dressing seasoning. Use hands to massage salt and oil on to leaves.

3. Put half your prepared bunch into your air fryer basket Close your air fryer lid, press Air Crisp at 390°F for about 2 minutes.

4. Lift lid and flip kale chips on to the other side to crisp evenly. Re set air crisp at 390°F for another 2 minutes.

5. Then remove and do the same for the 2nd half of your batch of prepared kale. Kale chips should be crispy on both sides. Enjoy immediately.

Blooming Onion

Preparation time: 2 hours

Cooking time: 20 minutes

Overall time: 2 hours 20 minutes

Serves: 1 to 3 people

Recipe Ingredients:

- large onion
- 2 eggs
- 2 tablespoons of milk
- 1 cup of panko bread crumbs
- 1 teaspoon of paprika
- 1 teaspoon of garlic powder
- Olive oil

Cooking Instructions:

1. Peel onion, cut off top. Place cut side down Starting ½ inch from the root, cut downward.

2. Cut 8 slices all the way around. Place onion Face down in ice cold water for about 2 hours.

3. Beat together egg and milk, in a separate bowl mix bread crumbs and seasonings. Coat onion with egg mixture make sure you get all petals.

4. Tip over to allow all access to drip off. Sprinkle panko all over the onion getting all of the onion.

5. Place in the basket of your Ninja Foodi or air Fryer. Spray with olive oil or cooking spray.

6. Cook on air crisp 390°F for about 10 minutes. Check if it's done if not crispy enough for your liking add an additional 5 minutes.

7. Serve immediately and Enjoy!

Fried Oreos

Preparation time: 5 minutes

Cooking time: 10 minutes

Overall time: 15 minutes

Serves: 2 to 4 people

Recipe Ingredients:

- 1 can of crescent rolls substitute crescent sheets
- 12 ea oreos

Cooking Instructions:

1. Roll out the crescent dough and pinch and roll any gaps closed.

2. Place cookies in three rows of four. Cut the dough in squares to match the cookie placement.

3. Pull the corners of the dough to the middle of the cookie. Pinch and close any gaps. Spray Ninja cooking basket lightly with nonstick spray.

4. Place oreos in single layer in the basket. Turn on Ninja Foodi to Air Crisp. Set to 350°F for about 6 minutes.

5. Server with powdered sugar, fudge sauce or marshmallow sauce.

Buffalo Cauliflower Bites

Preparation time: 40 minutes

Cooking time: 40 minutes

Overall time: 1 hour 20 minutes

Serves: 4 to 6 people

Recipe Ingredients:

- 2 heads of cauliflower, trimmed, cut in 2-inch florets
- 1 ½ cups of water, divided
- 1 ½ cups of cornstarch
- ½ cup of all-purpose flour
- 2 tsp. of baking powder
- 1 tsp. of garlic powder
- 1 tsp. of onion powder
- 1 tsp. of kosher salt
- 1 tsp. of black pepper
- 2 eggs
- 1/3 cup of buffalo wing sauce

Cooking Instructions:

1. Place cauliflower and ½ cup water into the pot. Assemble pressure lid, making sure the pressure release valve is in the seal position.

2. Select pressure and set to low, set time to 2 minutes. Select the start/stop button to begin.

3. When pressure cooking is complete, quick release the pressure by turning the pressure release valve to the vent position.

4. Carefully remove lid when unit has finished releasing pressure. Drain cauliflower and chill in refrigerator until cooled, for about 10 minutes.

5. Whisk together cornstarch, flour, baking powder, garlic powder, onion powder, salt, and pepper. Whisk in eggs and 1 cup water until batter is smooth.

6. Add chilled cauliflower to bowl with batter and gently toss until well coated. Transfer coated cauliflower to baking sheet and chill in freezer for 20 minutes.

7. Close crisping lid, preheat the unit by selecting air crisp, setting the temperature to 360°F, and setting the time to 5 minutes.

8. Meanwhile, arrange half the cauliflower in an even layer in the bottom of the cook & crisp basket.

9. After 5 minutes, place basket into the pot. Close crisping lid. Select air crisp, set temperature to 360°F, and set time to 20 minutes.

10. Select the start/stop button to begin. When first batch of cauliflower is crisp and golden, transfer to a bowl.

11. Repeat with remaining chilled cauliflower. When cooking is complete, microwave hot sauce for about 30 seconds.

12. Toss with cooked cauliflower and serve immediately.

Baked Brie

Preparation time: 10 minutes

Cooking time: 35 minutes

Overall time: 45 minutes

Serves: 2 to 4 people

Recipe Ingredients:

- ¼ cup of uncooked pancetta, diced
- 1 tbsp. of olive oil
- 1 medium onion, peeled, sliced
- ¼ cup of beef broth
- ½ tbsp. of balsamic vinegar
- 1 sheet frozen puff pastry dough, thawed
- 1 wheel (8 ounces) Brie cheese
- 1 egg, lightly beaten
- Crackers, for serving
- Apple slices, for serving

Cooking Instructions:

1. Select sear/sauté function and set to mid high mode. Select the start/stop button to begin.

2. Allow to preheat for about 5 minutes. After 5 minutes, place pancetta in the pot and cook for about 5 minutes.

3. Transfer cooked pancetta to a plate lined with paper towel and set aside. Add oil and onion to pot and cook for about 10 minutes, stirring occasionally.

4. Then add broth and balsamic vinegar and cook until all liquid is reduced. Remove onions from pot and set it aside.

5. Close crisping lid. Preheat the unit by selecting bake/roast, setting the temperature to 325°F, and setting the time to 5 minutes.

6. Select start/stop to begin. Meanwhile, place puff pastry dough on a flat surface. Place brie in the middle of dough, then top the brie with pancetta and onions.

7. Fold dough over the brie and toppings, sealing the edges. Place dough-wrapped brie seam side up in the ninja multi-purpose pan.

8. Brush with egg. Place pan on reversible rack, making sure rack is in the lower position. After unit has finished preheating, place rack with pan in pot.

9. Close crisping lid. Select the bake/roast function, set temperature to 325°F, and set time to 20 minutes.

10. Select the start/stop button to begin. Cooking is complete when pastry dough is golden brown.

11. Transfer baked brie to a platter and serve warm with crackers and apple slices.

Whole Roasted Sicilian Cauliflower

Preparation time 10 minutes

Cooking time: 13 minutes

Overall time: 23 minutes

Serves: 2 to 4 people

Recipe Ingredients:

- ½ cup of water
- 1 medium head cauliflower, leaves removed
- ¼ cup of olive oil
- 4 cloves of garlic, peeled, minced
- 2 tbsp. of capers, rinsed, minced
- 1 tsp. of crushed red pepper
- ½ cup of grated Parmesan cheese
- 1 tbsp. of fresh parsley, chopped, for garnish

Cooking Instructions:

1. Place water and cook & crisp basket in pot. With a knife, cut an x into the head of cauliflower, slicing about halfway down.

2. Place cauliflower into the basket. Assemble pressure lid, making sure the pressure release valve is in the seal position.

3. Select pressure and set to low. Set time to 3 minutes. Select the start/stop button to begin. In a small bowl, stir together olive oil, garlic, capers, and crushed red pepper.

4. When pressure cooking is complete, quick release the pressure by moving the pressure release valve to the vent position.

5. Carefully remove lid when unit has finished releasing pressure. Spread the oil mixture evenly over the cauliflower.

6. place some of it into the center of the cauliflower. Sprinkle parmesan cheese evenly over the cauliflower.

7. Close the crisping lid. Select air crisp, set temperature to 390°f, and set time to 10 minutes.

8. Select start/stop to begin. When cooking is complete, transfer cauliflower to a serving platter using a large spatula. Garnish with fresh parsley.

Sweet Potato Tots

Preparation time: 20 minutes

Cooking time: 23 minutes

Overall time: 43 minutes

Serves: 5 to 7

Recipe Ingredients:

- 3 sweet potatoes (about 1 3/4 pounds), peeled, cut in 1-inch cubes
- 4 sprigs of fresh thyme
- ¼ tsp. of ground garam masala or cinnamon
- 1 ½ tbsp. of kosher salt, divided
- 1 ½ cups of water
- ½ cup of cornstarch, divided
- 4 cups of panko bread crumbs
- 2 tsp. of ground cumin
- 1 tsp. of chili powder
- 1 tsp. of coarsely ground black pepper

Cooking Instructions:

1. Place sweet potatoes, thyme, garam masala or cinnamon, 1 teaspoon kosher salt, and water into the pot.

2. Assemble pressure lid, making sure the pressure release valve is in the seal position. Select pressure and set to high. Set time to 8 minutes.

3. Select the start/stop button to begin. When pressure cooking is complete, quick release the pressure by moving the pressure release valve to the vent position.

4. Carefully remove lid when unit has finished releasing pressure. Strain sweet potatoes in a colander.

5. Rinse pot and wipe dry, then place the cook & crisp basket in the pot. Transfer potatoes to a mixing bowl and mash well, add 2 tablespoons cornstarch.

6. Stir until smooth. In a separate bowl, stir together remaining salt, remaining cornstarch, bread crumbs, cumin, chili powder, and pepper.

7. Spray a large baking sheet with cooking spray. Form sweet potato mixture into 1-inch long cylindrical tots. Roll each tot in bread crumb mixture, coating evenly.

8. Place tots on baking sheet and place in freezer for 1 hour to set. Close crisping lid. Preheat unit by selecting air crisp.

9. Setting the temperature to 400°F, and setting the time to 5 minutes. Select the start/stop button to begin.

10. Once unit is preheated, spray the cook & crisp basket with cooking spray. Place tots in basket in a single layer.

11. Spray tots with cooking spray. Select air crisp, set temperature to 400°f, and set time to 15 minutes.

12. Select the start/stop button to begin. After 10 minutes, check for doneness. Cooking is complete when tots are golden brown and crispy.

13. Repeat steps 9 through 11 with remaining tots. When cooking is complete, tots are ready to serve.

Gobi Manchurian

Preparation time: 15 minutes

Cooking time: 35 minutes

Overall time: 50 minutes

Serves: 4 to 6 people

Recipe Ingredients:

- ½ cup of flour
- 3 tbsp. of cornstarch
- ½ tsp. of baking powder
- 1 tsp. of chili powder
- ¼ tsp. of kosher salt
- ¾ cup of water
- 1 head (4 cups) of cauliflower, cut in 2-inch florets
- 1 tsp. of sesame oil
- 1 tsp. of garlic, minced
- 1 tsp. of fresh ginger, minced
- 1 tsp. of chili paste
- 3 tbsp. of chili sauce
- 2 tbsp. of soy sauce
- 2 tbsp. of ketchup
- 2 tbsp. of fresh green onions, chopped, for garnish

Cooking Instructions:

1. In a large bowl, combine flour, cornstarch, baking powder, chili powder, and salt.

2. Whisk in water until a smooth, thick batter forms. Add cauliflower to batter and coat evenly. Transfer coated cauliflower to a sheet tray and freeze for 1 hour.

3. Select the sear/sauté function and set to mid high mode. Select start/stop to begin. Allow to preheat for about 5 minutes.

4. After 5 minutes, add oil, garlic, and ginger to pot and cook for 1 minute. And remaining ingredients, except green onions.

5. Cook until slightly thick, 2 to 3 minutes. Transfer sauce to a bowl and set aside. Wipe pot out with a paper towel.

6. After 1 hour, remove chilled cauliflower from freezer. Arrange half the florets in the cook & crisp basket and set it aside.

7. Close crisping lid and preheat the unit by selecting air crisp, setting the temperature to 360°F, and setting the time to 5 minutes.

8. Select the start/stop button to begin. After 5 minutes, place basket with cauliflower in pot.

9. Close crisping lid. Select air crisp, set temperature to 360°F, and set time to 16 minutes. Select the start/stop button to begin.

10. After 8 minutes, open lid, then lift basket and shake florets or toss them with silicone-tipped tongs.

11. Lower basket back into pot and close lid to resume cooking. Cooking is complete when florets are crispy and lightly browned.

12. Transfer them to a bowl and set it aside while you repeat the cooking process with remaining cauliflower.

13. Toss the cooked cauliflower with sauce. Garnish with green onions. Serve immediately.

Poutine

Preparation time 15 minutes

Cooking time: 45 minutes

Overall time: 1 hour

Serves: 2 to 4 people

Recipe Ingredients:

- 1 lb. of Idaho potatoes, sliced in 1/2-inch thick fries
- 6 cups of cold water
- 2 tbsp. of canola oil
- 4 tbsp. of unsalted butter
- ¼ cup of all-purpose flour
- 2 ½ cups of beef stock
- 1 ¼ cups of chicken stock
- 1 tbsp. of apple cider vinegar
- 2 tsp. of Worcestershire sauce
- 2 tbsp. of ketchup
- 1 tsp. of kosher salt
- ½ tsp. of ground black pepper
- 1 tbsp. of cornstarch and 1 tablespoon water, combined
- 1 ½ cups of cheese curds diced fresh mozzarella

Cooking Instructions:

1. Place fries and water in a large bowl and let soak for about 30 minutes. Place the Cook & Crisp Basket in the pot.

2. Close crisping lid and preheat the unit by selecting air crisp, setting the temperature to 390°f, and setting the time to 5 minutes.

3. While unit is preheating, drain fries thoroughly and pat dry with paper towels. Toss with oil. After 5 minutes, open the crisping lid and add fries to the basket.

4. Close lid. Select air crisp, set temperature to 390°f, and set time to 30 minutes. Select the start/stop button to begin.

5. Every 10 minutes, open lid, then lift basket and shake fries. Lower basket back into pot and close lid to resume cooking.

6. When cooking is complete, remove basket from pot and set it aside. Select sear/sauté and set to medium-high. Select the start/stop button to begin.

7. Allow to preheat for 5 minutes. After 5 minutes, melt butter in pot, then add flour, stirring continuously for 5 minutes until the mixture turns golden brown.

8. Slowly add beef and chicken stock, whisking quickly until smooth. Add vinegar, worcestershire sauce, ketchup, salt, and pepper.

9. Bring to a boil, then reduce temperature to medium, and cook for 10 minutes, whisking occasionally.

10. Stir in cornstarch mixture and simmer until sauce thickens. When cooking is complete, place fries on a serving platter.

11. Sprinkle with cheese and gravy and serve.

Toasted Ravioli

Preparation time: 15 minutes

Cooking time: 20 minutes

Overall time: 35 minutes

Serves: 2 to 4 people

Recipe Ingredients:

- 20 frozen ravioli
- 1 cup of all-purpose flour
- 3 eggs, whisked
- ¼ cup of olive oil
- 2 cups of Italian-style panko breadcrumbs
- 1 cup of marinara sauce

Cooking Instructions:

1. Place flour in a mixing bowl. Place eggs in another bowl.

2. In a third bowl, combine olive oil with panko breadcrumbs and mix thoroughly. Working in batches, toss ravioli in flour.

3. Shake off excess flour, then dip ravioli in eggs. Transfer ravioli to breadcrumbs and coat well and set it aside.

4. Place the cook & crisp basket in the pot. Close crisping lid. Preheat the unit by selecting air crisp, set the temperature to 375°F, and setting the time to 5 minutes.

5. After 5 minutes, open the crisping lid and place half the ravioli in the basket.close lid. Select the air crisp button, set temperature to 375°f, and set time to 10 minutes.

6. Select start/stop to begin. When cooking is complete, transfer ravioli to a serving dish. Place remaining ravioli in the basket and air crisp again.

7. When cooking is complete, serve ravioli with marinara sauce.

Falafel

Preparation time: 15 minutes

Cooking time: 45 minutes

Overall time: 1 hour

Serves: 2 to 4 people

Recipe Ingredients:

- 2 cans (15 oz. each) of chickpeas, drained, rinsed
- 1 small onion, peeled, chopped
- ¼ cup of bread crumbs
- ¼ cup of flat-leaf Italian parsley, chopped
- 2 tbsp. of lemon juice
- 2 cloves of garlic, peeled smashed
- 2 tsp. of ground cumin
- 1 tsp. of kosher salt
- 1 tsp. of ground coriander
- ½ tsp. of ground black pepper
- 5 tbsp. of extra virgin olive oil, divided
- 1 large egg

Cooking Instructions:

1. Spread chickpeas on a tray lined with paper towel and let air-dry while preparing other ingredients.

2. Combine onion, bread crumbs, parsley, lemon juice, garlic, cumin, salt, coriander, and black pepper in a food processor.

3. Pulse to combine until onions are finely minced. Add chickpeas, 3 tablespoons of oil, and egg, pulse just until chickpeas are broken down and mixture is combined.

4. Transfer mixture to a large bowl and stir to ensure it is evenly combined. Use a ¼-cup measuring cup to shape mixture into 16 patties.

5. Cover and refrigerate for at least 30 minutes. Brush patties on both sides with remaining oil. Place cook & crisp basket in pot and close crisping lid.

6. Preheat the unit by selecting air crisp, setting the temperature to 375° f, and setting the time to 5 minutes. Select the start/stop button to begin.

7. After 5 minutes, place half the patties in the basket, leaving ample space between them.

8. Close lid and select the air crisp function, set temperature to 375°F, and set time to 22 minutes. Select the start/stop button to begin.

9. After 11 minutes, use tongs to flip patties over. Close lid to resume cooking. When cooking is complete, remove patties and air crisp again with remaining patties.

10. Serve immediately and Enjoy!

Pot Stickers

Preparation time: 10 minutes

Cooking time: 30 minutes

Overall time: 40 minutes

Serves 4 to 6 people

Recipe Ingredients:

- 1 lb. of uncooked ground pork
- 1 cup of green cabbage, finely chopped
- ¾ cup of shiitake mushrooms (about 4 mushrooms), finely chopped
- 3 scallions, white and green parts minced
- 2 tbsp. of fresh ginger, minced
- 3 cloves of garlic, peeled, minced
- 1 tsp. of kosher salt
- 1 cup of low-sodium soy sauce
- 38 pot sticker wrappers (or round dumpling wrappers)
- 1 ¾ cups of water, divided
- 3 tbsp. of vegetable oil, divided

Cooking Instructions:

1. Combine pork, cabbage, mushrooms, scallions, ginger, garlic, salt, and 2 tablespoons of soy sauce in a large bowl.

2. Lay wrappers on a clean, dry surface, and place a scant tablespoon of filling in the center of each. Pour ¼ cup of water into a small bowl.

3. Use your finger or brush, spread water along half of each wrapper's circumference, fold wrappers over, pinch edges together to seal in a half-moon shape.

4. Place ½ cup of water in the pot. Place the reversible rack in the pot in the lower position, and spray with cooking spray.

5. Arrange a third of the pot stickers on rack, making sure they're sitting flat in 1 layer. Assemble pressure lid, make sure the pressure release valve is in the vent position.

6. Select steam and set time to 3 minutes. Select start/stop to begin. When steaming is complete, carefully remove lid.

7. Remove rack with pot stickers from the pot, and wipe out any remaining water. Select the sear/sauté function and set to high mode.

8. Select the start/stop button to begin and place 1 tablespoon oil in pot and heat until shimmering.

9. Using tongs, add steamed pot stickers, and cook until browned and crisp on both sides, about 2 minutes per side.

10. Select the start/stop button to turn off sear/sauté. Repeat the steps with remaining 2 batches of pot stickers.

11. When cooking is complete, serve hot with remaining ½ cup of soy sauce for dipping.

Black Bean Dip

Preparation time: 10 minutes

Cooking time: 15 minutes

Overall time: 25 minutes

Serves: 2 to 4 people

Recipe Ingredients:

- 2 cans (15.5 oz. each) of black beans, rinsed, drained
- 1 can (14.5 oz.) of diced or crushed tomatoes
- 1 onion, peeled, chopped
- 2 jalapeño peppers, chopped, seeds removed
- 4 cloves of garlic, peeled, chopped
- 2 tbsp. of extra virgin olive oil
- 1 ½ tsp. of kosher salt
- 1 tsp. of ground cumin
- 1 tsp. of chili powder
- ½ tsp. of smoked paprika
- 2 tbsp. of fresh lime juice, plus more as needed
- ½ cup of fresh cilantro leaves, chopped
- 1 cup of shredded Monterey Jack cheese (optional)

Cooking Instructions:

1. Place beans, tomatoes, onion, jalapeño peppers, garlic, oil, salt, cumin, chili powder, and smoked paprika in the pot.

2. Assemble the pressure lid, making sure the pressure release valve is in the seal position. Select pressure and set to high. Set time to 5 minutes.

3. Select the start/stop button to begin. When pressure cooking is complete, quick release the pressure by moving the pressure release valve to the vent position.

4. Carefully remove lid when unit has finished releasing pressure. For a rustic texture, mash with a potato masher.

5. For a smoother dip, blend with an immersion blender until smooth. Stir in lime juice and cilantro. Serve warm, or at room temperature.

DESSERT RECIPES

Apple Crisp

Preparation time: 15 minutes

Cooking time: 40 minutes

Overall time: 55 minutes

Serves: 6 to 8 people

Recipe Ingredients:

- 2 ½ lb. of honey crisp apples, thinly sliced
- ½ cup of white sugar
- ½ tablespoon of gluten-free all-purpose flour
- 1 teaspoon of ground cinnamon
- 1 teaspoon of ground nutmeg
- ½ cup of water

Topping:

- 1 cup of gluten-free old-fashioned oats
- 1 cup of gluten-free all-purpose flour
- 1 cup of brown sugar, packed
- ¼ teaspoon of baking powder
- ¼ teaspoon of baking soda
- ½ cup of butter, softened
- Vanilla ice cream, optional

Cooking Instructions:

1. Place the sliced apples evenly in the pot of the Ninja Foodi.

2. In a small bowl, combine the sugar, flour, cinnamon, and nutmeg. Evenly pour this over the apples.

3. Pour the water over the apples. In a small bowl, combine the oats, flour, brown sugar, baking powder, and baking soda.

4. Mix in the softened butter. This should be a crumble mixture. Evenly add this to the top of the apples.

5. Shut the lid that is attached to the Ninja Foodi. Bake for about 40 minutes at 350°F. Serve warm with a side of vanilla ice cream.

Mini Apple Tarts

Preparation time: 5 minutes

Cooking time: 15 minutes

Overall time: 20 minutes

Serves: 4 to 6 people

Recipe Ingredients:

- 6 tart shells, thawed
- 1 cup of apple pie filling
- ½ teaspoon of cinnamon
- Dash nutmeg
- Whipped topping or ice cream, as desired

Cooking Instructions:

1. Place the tart shells in the bowl of the Foodi.

2. Air crisp them for about 5 to 7 minutes on 400°F. My suggestion here is to keep an eye on them as they will bake very quickly and get brown fast.

3. When they are baked through and starting to get some color, remove and let it cool. While shells are baking, cut down the slices of apples in the filling if they are long.

4. You want small pieces of apple in this filling. Add the spices to the apple pie filling and mix well.

5. When the shells have cooled, divide evenly and spoon the filling into each of the tart shells. Place the shells onto the trivet rack that came with the appliance.

6. Putting them on the rack will make for an even bake on all the tarts, and make it easier to remove them all at once. Sprinkle with a little extra cinnamon.

7. Air crisp the tarts again until the tops of the filling is caramelized and the tarts are a nice golden brown.

8. Remove and allow to cool slightly. Dollop with whipped cream or ice cream. Enjoy!

Ninja Cake

Preparation time: 10 minutes

Cooking time: 20 minutes

Overall time: 30 minutes

Serves: 4 to 6 people

Recipe Ingredients:

- 1 box cake mix we used carrot cake boxed cake
- Ingredients to make batter

Cooking Instructions:

1. Lower down a trivet, one with handles. Prepare cake mix as directed. Spray nonstick spray into your 9" bundt pan and pour your batter in,

2. It will fit an entire prepared box of cake. Put bundt pan on trivet and close lid. Press bake, 325°F for about 20 minutes.

3. Lift lid when done and allow to sit for about 5 minutes. Lift out and put on cooling rack outside of pot.

4. Once cooled put a plate on top and gently flip over, cake should fall out easily. Warm frosting and pour on top. Slice and serve.

Lemon Cream Cheese Dump Cake

Preparation time: 5 minutes

Cooking time: 30 minutes

Overall time: 35 minutes

Serves: 4 to 6 people

Recipe Ingredients:

- 1 can (16 oz.) lemon pie filling
- 1 Package (15 oz.) of yellow cake mix
- 4 oz. of cream cheese cut into small pieces
- ½ cup of butter cut into thin slices

Cooking Instructions:

1. Spray pot with nonstick cooking spray. Spread lemon pie filling in the bottom of the pot.

2. Top with half of the cake mix, dot with cream cheese and cover with the remaining cake mix.

3. Top with butter in a single layer, trying to cover all areas of cake mix leaving none exposed.

4. Close the crisping lid and select the bake/roast function and set temperature to 350 degrees and set time to 30 minutes.

5. Select Start, open the crisping lid while it is cooking to check on its progress. You will want to check around 25 minutes to make sure the top is not browning much.

6. Test with toothpick at 30 minutes. It should come out clean. Scoop out with a big spoon.

7. Serve it warm or cold. With ice cream or without.

Zeppole

Preparation time: 30 minutes

Cooking time: 25 minutes

Overall time: 55 minutes

Serves: 10 to 12 people

Recipe Ingredients:

- ¼ cup of water
- 1 tsp. of active dry yeast
- 2 tbsp. of sugar plus 1 teaspoon sugar, divided
- 2 cups of all-purpose flour
- ½ cup of whole-milk ricotta cheese
- 1 large egg
- Zest of 1 orange
- 1 tsp. of vanilla extract
- ¾ tsp. of kosher salt
- ¼ tsp. of freshly grated nutmeg
- 1 ½ sticks (3/4 cup) of unsalted butter, softened, divided
- Confectioners' sugar, for dusting

Cooking Instructions:

1. Warm water to 110° F, then combine with yeast and 1 teaspoon of sugar in the bowl of a stand mixer and let sit until mixture becomes foamy, for about 5 minutes.

2. Add flour, ricotta, egg, orange zest, vanilla, salt, nutmeg, and remaining 2 tablespoons sugar, attach bowl to stand mixer fitted with dough hook attachment.

3. Mix on low speed until the dough forms. Gradually add ½ cup of butter, one tablespoon at a time, occasionally stopping mixer to scrape down sides of bowl.

4. Increase speed to medium and beat until dough is cohesive, smooth, and glossy, for about 4 minutes. If necessary, scrape dough from hook and sides of bowl.

5. Remove bowl from mixer, cover with plastic wrap and let rise at room temperate for about 2 hours.

6. Transfer dough to a lightly floured surface and shape into a smooth ball. Divide into 12 equal portions and roll into tight balls.

7. Place on a baking sheet and let sit covered at room temperature for about 30 minutes. After 30 minutes, close crisping lid.

8. Preheat the unit by selecting air crisp, setting the temperature to 360°F, and setting the time to 3 minutes. Select start/stop to begin.

9. Melt remaining ¼ cup of butter. Brush half the dough balls with melted butter and place them in the cook & crisp basket.

10. Reserve unused butter, once unit has preheated, place basket in pot. Close lid. Select air crisp, set temperature to 360°F, and set time to 12 minutes.

11. Select the start/stop button to begin. Cooking is complete when zeppole are deep golden brown.

12. Remove them from basket, brush again with melted butter, and sprinkle with confectioners' sugar. Repeat the 8 with remaining dough balls.

13. Serve warm.

Mexican Pot du Crème

Preparation time: 10 minutes

Cooking time: 10 minutes

Overall time: 20 minutes

Serves: 4 to 6 people

Recipe Ingredients:

- 1 ½ cups of heavy cream
- ½ cup of whole milk
- 2 tbsp. of coffee-flavored liqueur
- ½ tsp. of ground cinnamon
- ¼ tsp. of ancho chili powder
- 5 egg yolks
- ¼ cup of sugar
- Pinch kosher salt
- 2 bars (4 ounces each) bittersweet chocolate, melted
- 1 cup of water
- Whipped cream, for serving

Cooking Instructions:

1. Select the sear/sauté function and set to mid high mode. Select start/stop to begin. Allow to preheat for about 5 minutes.

2. Add heavy cream, milk, liqueur, cinnamon, and chili powder to pot. Bring mixture to a simmer, then select start/stop to turn off sear/sauté.

3. In a large bowl, whisk together egg yolks, sugar, and salt. Then slowly whisk the warm cream mixture into the egg mixture.

4. Add melted chocolate and whisk until fully incorporated. Divide mixture between 6 (6 oz.) ramekins.

5. Tightly wrap each ramekin with aluminum foil. Add water to pot. Place the reversible rack in pot, making sure rack is in the lower position.

6. Place 4 ramekins on rack, then carefully stack the remaining ramekins on top. Assemble pressure lid, make sure the pressure release valve is in the seal position.

7. Select pressure and set to high. Set time to 8 minutes. Select the start/stop button to begin.

8. when pressure cooking is complete, allow pressure to release naturally for about 10 minutes.

9. After 10 minutes, quick release any remaining pressure by moving the pressure release valve to the vent position.

10. Carefully remove lid when unit has finished releasing pressure. remove ramekins from pot with tongs, remove foil.

11. Place ramekins in refrigerator to cool completely before serving. Once cooled, serve with whipped cream.

Hot Peach & Blackberry Cobbler

Preparation time: 10 minutes

Cooking time: 20 minutes

Overall time: 30 minutes

Serves: 4 to 6 people

Recipe Ingredients:

- 4 cups (24 oz.) of frozen sliced peaches
- 2 cups (10 oz.) of frozen blackberries
- Juice of 2 Meyer lemons (about 1/3 cup juice)
- Zest of 1 lemon
- 2/3 cup of sugar, plus more to taste
- 5 tbsp. of cornstarch
- 1 tsp. of ground cinnamon
- 2 cups of water

Topping:

- 1 ½ cups of flour
- 1 cup of light brown sugar, packed
- 1 tbsp. of ground cinnamon
- ¼ tsp. of fine-grain sea salt
- 2/3 cup of unsalted butter, melted
- 1 ½ tsp. of vanilla extract
- Vanilla ice cream, for serving

Cooking Instructions:

1. Place peaches and blackberries mixture into the Ninja multi-purpose pan.

2. In a separate bowl, stir together lemon juice, lemon zest, sugar, cornstarch, and 1 teaspoon cinnamon; pour over the fruit and stir gently.

3. Allow it to sit for about 5 minutes, place pan on reversible rack, making sure rack is in the lower position.

4. Pour water into the pot and add rack with pan to the pot. Assemble pressure lid, making sure the pressure release valve is in the seal position.

5. Select pressure and set to high. Set time to 7 minutes. Select the start/stop button to begin.

6. While fruit is cooking, make the topping by stirring together the flour, brown sugar, 1 tablespoon cinnamon, and salt in a medium bowl.

7. Add melted butter and vanilla and stir to combine. Mix until the butter is well incorporated.

8. It will come together in lumps or balls, and will have a crumbly texture and set it aside.

9. When pressure cooking is complete, allow pressure to natural release for about 10 minutes.

10. After 10 minutes, quick release remaining pressure by moving the pressure release valve to the vent position.

11. Carefully remove lid when unit has finished releasing pressure, carefully stir the fruit mixture, then allow to rest in the pot for about 10 to 15 minutes to thicken.

12. After 10 minutes, evenly spread topping over the fruit mixture. Close crisping lid. Select the air crisp function, set temperature to 350°f, and set time to 10 minutes.

13. Select start/stop to begin. When cooking is complete, let cool slightly and serve with vanilla ice cream.

Cranberry Oat Bars

Preparation time: 15 minutes

Cooking time: 30 minutes

Overall time: 45 minutes

Serves: 6 to 8 people

Recipe Ingredients:

- 1 cup of all-purpose flour
- 1 cup of quick-cooking rolled oats
- 1/3 cup of brown sugar
- ¼ tsp. of baking soda
- 1 stick (1/2 cup) of butter, room temperature
- 1 cup of whole cranberry sauce

Cooking Instructions:

1. In mixing bowl, combine flour, oats, brown sugar, and baking soda.

2. Use your hands or a pastry cutter, blend butter into mixture until it resembles coarse crumbs.

3. Close crisping lid. Preheat the unit by selecting bake/roast, setting the temperature to 325°F, and setting the time to 5 minutes. Select the start/stop button to begin.

4. Meanwhile, reserve 1 cup crumb mixture; set aside. Grease the ninja multi-purpose pan. Press remaining mixture into the bottom of the pan.

5. Spread cranberry sauce over crumb mixture. Sprinkle 1 cup reserved mixture on top. Place pan on reversible rack, making sure rack is in the lower position.

6. Once unit is preheated, place rack with pan in pot. Close crisping lid. Select bake/roast, set temperature to 325°F, and set time to 30 minutes.

7. Select start/stop to begin. When cooking is complete, remove rack with pan from pot. Let cool completely before cutting into bars and serving.

Citrus Olive Oil Cake

Preparation time: 10 minutes

Cooking time: 40 minutes

Overall time: 50 minutes

Serves: 6 to 8 people

Recipe Ingredients

- 4 eggs
- 1 cup of sugar
- 1 cup of extra virgin olive oil
- Juice and zest of 1 orange
- Juice and zest of 1 lemon
- 1 cup of all-purpose flour
- 1 tbsp. of baking powder
- ¼ tsp. of kosher salt
- Powdered sugar, for garnish

Cooking Instructions:

1. In a food processor, combine eggs, sugar, olive oil, zests, and juices. Process until incorporated.

2. In a separate mixing bowl, whisk together flour, baking powder, and salt. Add dry ingredients to the food processor, about 1/3 at a time.

3. Pulse only to combine, scraping down sides. Make sure to avoid over-mixing. Generously grease bottom of the Ninja multi-purpose pan with olive oil.

4. Add batter to pan and place pan on reversible rack, making sure the rack is in the lower orientation. Close the crisping lid.

5. Preheat the unit by selecting bake/roast, setting the temperature to 325°F, and setting the time to 3 minutes. Select the start/stop button to begin.

6. After 3 minutes, open lid and place rack with pan in pot. Close the crisping lid. Select bake/roast, set temperature to 325°F, and set time to 40 minutes.

7. Select start/stop to begin. Check for doneness after 35 minutes. Cooking is complete when a toothpick inserted in center comes out clean.

8. When cooking is complete, carefully remove rack with pan from pot and place on a cooling rack.

9. Allow cake to cool at least 15 minutes before removing from pan.

10. Let cool completely before serving. Garnish with powdered sugar, if desired.

Caramel Apple Hand Pies

Preparation time: 45 minutes

Cooking time: 24 minutes

Overall time: 1 hour 10 minutes

Serves: 6 to 8 people

Recipe Ingredients

Soup:

- 1 ¼ cups of all-purpose flour
- ½ tsp. of kosher salt
- ½ tsp. of sugar
- 1 stick (1/2 cup) of unsalted butter, cold, cut in cubes
- 3 tbsp. of ice water

Quesadillas:

- 1 granny Smith apple, peeled, cored, diced
- 1 tsp. of lemon juice
- 1 tbsp. of sugar
- ½ tsp. of ground cinnamon
- 2 tbsp. of toffee bits
- Egg wash (1 egg whisked with 1 tablespoon water)
- Caramel syrup, for drizzling (optional)

Cooking Instructions:

1. To make the dough for the crust, place flour, salt, and sugar in a food processor. Pulse to combine. Add butter and pulse until dough resembles coarse meal.

2. Add 2 tablespoons ice water. Pulse until dough comes together, adding more water if needed. Place dough on a lightly floured work surface and form into a disk.

3. Wrap in plastic wrap and refrigerate for about 30 minutes. Meanwhile, prepare the filling by combining apples, lemon juice, sugar, cinnamon.

4. Toffee bits in a small bowl and set it aside. Place cook & crisp basket in pot. Close crisping lid.

5. Preheat the unit by selecting air crisp, setting the temperature to 325°f, and setting the time to 5 minutes. Select the start/stop button to begin.

6. Meanwhile, remove dough from refrigerator. Roll it out onto a lightly floured surface, in a 1/4-inch thick rectangle.

7. Using a 3-inch round biscuit cutter or drinking glass, cut out 16 circles of dough. Place 1 teaspoon of apple filling in the center of 8 of the dough circles

8. Leave a border around the filling. Brush the edges with egg wash. Place a second dough circle on top of each and seal the edges, using a fork to crimp.

9. Brush the top of each pie with egg wash. Open the crisping lid and add 4 pies to basket, making sure they don't overlap.

10. Close crisping lid. Select air crisp, set temperature to 325°F, and set time to 12 minutes. Select start/stop to begin.

11. After 8 minutes, open lid and flip pies over. Close lid to resume cooking. When cooking is complete, remove pies.

12. Repeat steps 8 through 10 with the remaining 4 pies. Let pies cool before serving. Drizzle with caramel syrup, if desired.

Bananas Foster

Preparation time: 5 minutes

Cooking time: 5 minutes

Overall time: 10 minutes

Serves: 2 to 4 people

Recipe Ingredients:

- ½ cup of butter
- 1 cup of dark brown sugar
- 1 tsp. of ground cinnamon
- 4 small bananas, peeled, cut half lengthwise, then cut in half again
- ½ cup of rum
- Vanilla ice cream, for serving

Cooking Instructions:

1. Select the sear/sauté function and set to mid high mode.

2. Select the start/stop button to begin. Allow to preheat for about 5 minutes. After 5 minutes, place butter, brown sugar, and cinnamon in the pot.

3. Stir until butter and brown sugar dissolve. Add bananas to pot. Spoon the sauce over them and cook until their edges start to soften and mixture begins to bubble.

4. Stir in the rum. Cook for another 2 minutes. Select start/stop to turn off unit. Serve bananas immediately with vanilla ice cream.

Arroz Con Leche

Preparation time: 5 minutes

Cooking time: 7 minutes

Overall time: 12 minutes

Serves: 4 to 6 people

Recipe Ingredients:

- 1 cup of long grain white rice
- 3 1/3 cups of whole milk, cold, divided
- ¼ cup of granulated sugar
- 2 strips lime zest
- 2 cinnamon sticks
- 1/8 tsp. of kosher salt
- ½ can (7 oz.) of sweetened condensed milk
- Ground cinnamon, for garnish

Cooking Instructions:

1. Place rice, 3 cups milk, sugar, lime zest, cinnamon sticks, and salt into the pot. Stir to combine.

2. Assemble pressure lid, making sure the pressure release valve is in the seal position. Select pressure and set to high mode. Set time to 2 minutes.

3. Select the start/stop button to begin. When pressure cooking is complete, allow pressure to release naturally for about 10 minutes.

4. After 10 minutes, quick release any remaining pressure by moving the pressure release valve to the vent position.

5. Carefully remove lid when unit has finished releasing pressure. Add sweetened condensed milk to the pot and stir to incorporate. Select sear/sauté and set to med.

6. Select the start/stop button to begin. Allow to simmer for about 5 minutes, stirring frequently. Carefully remove pot to a heat-safe surface.

7. Stir in the remaining milk and allow to cool for about 15 minutes. Serve warm after 15 minutes, or cool to room temperature.

8. Refrigerate and serve cold, garnished with ground cinnamon.

Chocolate Chip Skillet Cookie

Preparation time: 10 minutes

Cooking time: 23 minutes

Overall time: 33 minutes

Serves: 2 to 4 people

Recipe Ingredients:

- 1 ½ cup of all-purpose flour
- ½ tsp. of baking soda
- ½ tsp. of kosher salt
- 1 stick (1/2 cup) of unsalted butter, softened, plus more for greasing
- 6 tbsp. of granulated sugar
- 6 tbsp. of packed brown sugar
- ½ tsp. of vanilla extract
- 1 large egg
- 1 cup of semi-sweet chocolate chips
- ½ cup of chopped walnuts, pecans, or almonds, if desired

Cooking Instructions:

1. Close crisping lid. Preheat the unit by selecting bake/roast, setting the temperature to 325°F, and setting the time to 5 minutes. Select the start/stop button to begin.

2. While unit is preheating, whisk together flour, baking soda, and salt in a mixing bowl.

3. In a separate mixing bowl, beat together the butter, sugars, and vanilla until creamy. Add egg and beat until smooth and fully incorporated.

4. Slowly add the dry ingredients to the egg mixture, about 1/3 at a time. Use a rubber spatula to scrape down the sides so all dry ingredients get incorporated.

5. Make sure not to over-mix, or the cookie will become dense when baked. Fold the chocolate chips and nuts into the cookie dough until they are evenly distributed.

6. Generously grease the bottom of the ninja multi-purpose pan. Add the cookie dough to the pan, making sure it is evenly distributed.

7. Once unit has preheated, place the pan onto the reversible rack, making sure rack is in the lower position. Place rack with pan in pot. Close crisping lid.

8. Select the bake/roast function, set temperature to 325°F, and set time to 23 minutes. Select start/stop to begin.

9. When cooking is complete, allow cookie to cool for about 5 minutes. Serve warm with toppings of your choice.

Peach Cherry Crumble

Preparation time: 10 minutes

Cooking time: 22 minutes

Overall time: 32 minutes

Serves: 2 to 4 people

Recipe Ingredients:

- 1 package (16 oz.) of frozen peaches
- 1 cup of frozen cherries
- 2 tbsp. of cornstarch
- 1 cup of water, divided
- 1 tsp. of fresh lemon juice
- 3 tbsp. of sugar

Topping:

- ½ cup of flour
- ½ cup of rolled oats
- 2/3 cup of brown sugar
- 2 tbsp. of granulated sugar
- 1/3 cup of butter, cut in pieces
- 1 tsp. of ground cinnamon

Cooking Instructions:

1. Place peaches and cherries into the Ninja multi-purpose pan.

2. In a separate bowl, stir together the cornstarch, ½ cup water, lemon juice, and sugar; pour over the fruit.

3. Place pan on reversible rack, making sure rack is in the lower position, and cover pan with foil. Pour 1/2 cup water into pot and add rack to the pot.

4. Assemble pressure lid, making sure the pressure release valve is in the seal position. Select pressure and set to high. Set time to 10 minutes.

5. Select the start/stop button to begin. In a separate bowl, combine all topping ingredients until incorporated.

6. When pressure cooking is complete, quick release the pressure by moving the pressure release valve to the vent position.

7. Carefully remove lid when unit has finished releasing pressure. Remove foil and evenly spread topping over the fruit. Close crisping lid.

8. Select air crisp, set temperature to 400°f, and set time to 12 minutes. Select start/stop to begin.

9. Cook until top is browned and fruit is bubbling. When cooking is complete, remove rack with pan from pot and serve.

Berry Upside Down Cake

Preparation time: 15 minutes

Cooking time: 55 minutes

Overall time: 1 hour 10 minutes

Serves: 6 to 8 people

Recipe Ingredients:

- 1 bag (12 oz.) of frozen cherries
- 1 bag (12 oz.) of frozen blueberries
- 1 stick (1/2 cup) of butter, divided
- 2 tbsp. of lemon juice
- 2 tsp. of cornstarch
- 1 cup of plus 3 tablespoons sugar, divided
- 2 cups of all-purpose flour
- ¼ tsp. of baking soda
- 2 tsp. of baking powder
- ½ tsp. of kosher salt
- 3 large eggs
- 1 cup of sour cream

Toppings:

- Crème Fraiche
- Mascarpone
- Whipped Cream
- Vanilla Ice Cream

Cooking Instructions:

1. Place frozen fruit, 3 tablespoons butter, lemon juice, cornstarch, and 3 tablespoons sugar in the pot; stir to combine.

2. Assemble pressure lid, making sure the pressure release valve is in the seal position. Select pressure and set to high. Set time to 5 minutes.

3. Select the start/stop button to begin. When pressure cooking is complete, allow pressure to natural release for about 5 minutes.

4. After 5 minutes, quick release remaining pressure by moving the pressure release valve to the vent position.

5. Carefully remove lid when unit has finished releasing pressure. Select sear/sauté and set to mid high.

6. Allow liquid to simmer for about 10 minutes, until it begins to thicken and look syrupy. Remove pot from unit and place on a heat-resistant surface.

7. Let cool for 15 minutes. Meanwhile, place all-purpose flour, remaining sugar, baking soda, baking powder, and salt into a mixing bowl. Whisk to incorporate.

8. Melt remaining 5 tablespoons of butter in a separate mixing bowl, then whisk in eggs and sour cream. Slowly add flour mixture to egg mixture.

9. Beat until batter is thick and smooth. Gently dollop and smooth batter evenly over the top of the cooled berry mixture.

10. Close crisping lid. Select air crisp, set temperature to 325°F, and set time to 40 minutes. Select start/stop to begin.

11. When cooking is complete, remove pot from unit and place on a heat-resistant surface.

12. Let it cool for about 15 to 20 minutes before serving with toppings of your choice.

KETOGENIC RECIPES

Spinach & Artichoke Dip

Preparation time: 5 minutes

Cooking time: 15 minutes

Overall time: 20 minutes

Servings: 6 to 8 people

Recipe Ingredients:

- 8 ounces of mozzarella cheese
- 8 ounces of parmesan cheese
- 8 ounces of pepper jack cheese
- 8 ounces of cream cheese
- ½ cup of mayonnaise
- ½ cup of chicken broth
- ½ cup of sour cream
- 10 ounces of frozen spinach- thawed
- 1 tbsp. of minced garlic
- 1 (14 ounces) can of artichokes drained

Cooking Instructions:

1. Add garlic to Ninja Foodi, add chicken broth, mayonnaise, sour cream add spinach, cream cheese, artichokes and stir until combined.

2. Close pressure cooker lid- move valve to "seal" position, cook on high pressure for about 4 minutes.

3. Quick release pressure and remove lid, stir and add cheese

Whole Cauliflower

Preparation time: 5 minute

Cooking time: 10 minutes

Overall time: 15 minutes

Serves: 2 to 4 people

Recipe Ingredients:

- Medium cauliflower head
- Olive oil - either spritz or to baste
- Seasoning - like garlic salt

Cooking Instructions:

1. Add one cup of water in the bowl of the Ninja, add your inner pot.

2. Add your pressure cooker lid and Seal. Pressure cook on Low for about 3 minutes. Quickly Release pressure.

3. Once pressure is released, remove the pressure cooker lid. Dump out excess Water Spritz or baste on olive oil to head of cauliflower.

4. Add any seasoning you like. Finish your cauliflower by Air Frying 10 minutes, until slightly golden and flavored.

5. Remove with tongs and carefully cut or enjoy as is. Should be fork tender!

Casserole

Preparation time: 10 minutes

Cooking time: 15 minutes

Overall time: 25 minutes

Serves: 2 to 4 people

Recipe Ingredients

- 1 pound of ground sausage
- ¼ cup of diced white onion
- 1 diced green bell pepper
- 8 whole eggs, beaten
- ½ cup of shredded Colby jack cheese
- 1 teaspoon of fennel seed
- ½ teaspoon of garlic salt

Cooking Instructions:

1. If you are using the Ninja Foodi, use the sauté function to brown the sausage in the pot of the foodi.

2. Add in the onion and pepper and cook along with the ground sausage until the veggies are soft and the sausage is cooked.

3. Using the 8.75-inch pan, spray it with non-stick cooking spray. Place the ground sausage mixture on the bottom of the pan. Top evenly with cheese.

4. Pour the beaten eggs evenly over the cheese and sausage. Add fennel seed and garlic salt evenly over the eggs.

5. Place the rack in the low position in the Ninja Foodi, and then place the pan on top. Set to Air Crisp for about 15 minutes at 390°F.

6. Carefully remove, serve immediately and enjoy!

Zucchini Chips

Preparation time: 5 minutes

Cooking time: 12 minutes

Overall time: 17 minutes

Serves: 3 to 5 people

Recipe Ingredients

- 1 zucchini medium size, cut into chips
- 1 eggs beaten
- ¾ cup of panko crumbs
- ¼ cup of Parmesan cheese
- Olive oil spray

Cooking Instructions:

1. Slice zucchini, on the thinner side, in a small bowl, scramble the egg. In another bowl, add the panko bread crumbs & parmesan cheese.

2. Mix to combine. Gently dip the zucchini slices into the egg mixture. Than dip into the panko crumb mixture and coat both sides.

3. Spray your crisper basket with Olive Oil Spray. Place zucchini coins in a single layer into your basket. Spray tops of the slices with oil spray. Close the crisping lid.

4. Select the Air Crisp function, set temperature to 400°F degrees, set the time to 12 minutes. After 8 minutes, flip your zucchini slices and spray the tops with olive oil.

5. Cook the remaining 4 minutes and ENJOY!

Oatmeal

Preparation time: 5 minutes

Cooking time: 25 minutes

Overall time: 30 minutes

Serves: 2 to 4 people

Recipe Ingredients:

- 1 cup of rolled oats or old-fashioned oats (gluten-free or regular)
- 1 cup of milk
- 1 cup of water
- ¼ teaspoon of ground cinnamon
- steel-cut oats (choose this or rolled oats)
- 1 cup of steel-cut oats or gluten-free steel-cut oats
- 1 cup of milk
- 2 cups of water
- ¼ teaspoon of ground cinnamon

Toppings:

- Fruit (strawberries, blueberries, peaches, etc)
- Chocolate chips
- Nuts
- Dried cranberries
- Chia seeds
- Flax seeds
- Maple syrup
- Brown sugar

Cooking Instructions:

1. Depending on which one you choose to make either Rolled Oats or Steel Cut Oats, add all ingredients to the pot of the Ninja Foodi.

2. Secure the pressure cooker lid to the Ninja Foodi, set the nozzle to "seal". If you are using rolled oats, set to pressure cook for about 3 minutes on high mode.

3. If you are using steel-cut oats, set to pressure cook for about 6 minutes on high mode. Once the time is up, release the steam naturally for about 20 minutes.

4. After 20 minutes, turn the nozzle to vent and release the remaining steam. Serve with your choice of toppings.

Cheeseburger Soup

Preparation time: 10 minutes

Cooking time: 20 minutes

Overall time: 30 minutes

Serves: 6 to 8 people

Recipe Ingredients:

- 1 pound of ground beef
- ½ teaspoon of kosher salt and black pepper
- 2 (300g) sweet onions, diced
- 5 (400g) baby Yukon gold potatoes, cubed
- 3 (150g) carrots, sliced
- 4 cloves (20g) of garlic, minced
- 2 tablespoons of chopped parsley
- 1 tablespoon of ground mustard
- ½ teaspoon of dill weed, optional
- 2 cups (480g) of low sodium chicken broth
- 1 cups (227g) of fat free Greek yogurt
- ½ cup (56g) of cheddar powder

Cooking Instructions:

1. Use the sauté function of your pressure cooker to brown the ground beef.

2. Add salt and pepper halfway through cooking. When the beef is fully cooked, add the potatoes, carrots, onion, and garlic, stirring everything together.

3. Add the parsley, ground mustard, dill weed, and chicken broth, stirring everything together once more.

4. Cook on high pressure for 10 minutes with quick release pressure. While the soup cooks, mix the cheddar powder and Greek yogurt together.

5. Add the yogurt and cheese mixture to the soup once you've vented. Stir well and leave the pressure cooker on its keep warm function.

Steak Wrapped Asparagus

Preparation time: 10 minutes

Cooking time: 10 minutes

Overall time: 20 minutes

Serves: 4 to 6 people

Recipe Ingredients:

- 1 lb. of asparagus, trimmed
- 2 cups of grape tomatoes, halved
- 1 ½ lb. of skirt steak or flank steak, thinly sliced
- 4 tablespoons of balsamic vinegar
- 4 tablespoons of olive oil
- 1 clove of garlic, crushed
- 1 teaspoon of salt
- Olive oil cooking spray

Cooking Instructions:

1. Spray the basket of the Ninja Foodi lightly with olive oil spray. Slice the steak against the grain into 6 pieces, as evenly as possible.

2. In a small bowl, combine the vinegar, oil, garlic, and salt. Just lightly mix it. It's not going to fully combine.

3. Take about 3 asparagus and place them in 1 slice of steak, roll it up and place it in the basket of the Ninja Foodi.

4. Continue this process for all of the steak. For this recipe, the basket will fit 3 at a time. Once there are 3 in the basket, add in half of the tomatoes.

5. Using a brush, brush the steaks and the vegetables with the oil and vinegar mixture.

6. Cook using the air crisp function at 390°F for about 10 minutes using the attached lid with the Ninja Foodi.

7. Carefully remove and repeat the process for the remaining 3 steaks. Serve the steak wrapped asparagus with tomatoes.

Steak and Vegetable Bowls

Preparation time: 5 minutes

Cooking time: 15 minutes

Overall time: 20 minutes

Serves: 4 to 6 people

Recipe Ingredients:

- 2 kc strip steaks
- 1 cup of red bell pepper, diced
- 1 cup of green bell pepper, diced
- 1 cup of yellow squash, diced
- 1 cup of mushroom, sliced
- ¼ cup of white onion, diced
- ½ tablespoon of steak seasoning
- Olive oil cooking spray

Cooking Instructions:

1. Cut the steak into smaller cubed chunks. Spray the basket of the ninja foodi basket.

2. Place the steaks and vegetables in the air fryer or ninja foodi basket. Sprinkle evenly with the seasoning. Spray with olive oil spray.

3. Cook for about 7 minutes on 390ºF. Carefully open the lid and stir and mix the ingredients, coat with additional olive oil spray.

4. Cook for an additional 8 minutes at 390ºF or until done to your preference.

Casserole

Preparation time: 10 minutes

Cooking time: 15 minutes

Overall time: 25 minutes

Serves: 6 to 8 people

Recipe Ingredients:

- 1 pound of ground sausage
- ¼ cup of diced white onion
- 1 diced green bell pepper
- 8 whole eggs, beaten
- ½ cup of shredded Colby jack cheese
- 1 teaspoon of fennel seed
- ½ teaspoon garlic salt

Cooking Instructions:

1. If you are using the Ninja Foodi, use the sauté function to brown the sausage in the pot of the foodi.

2. Add in the onion and pepper and cook along with the ground sausage until the veggies are soft and the sausage is cooked.

3. Using the 8.75-inch pan or the Air Fryer pan, spray it with non-stick cooking spray. Place the ground sausage mixture on the bottom of the pan.

4. Top evenly with cheese. Pour the beaten eggs evenly over the cheese and sausage. Add fennel seed and garlic salt evenly over the eggs.

5. Place the rack in the low position in the Ninja Foodi, and then place the pan on top. Set to Air Crisp for about 15 minutes at 390°F.

6. Carefully remove and serve.

Chili Recipe No Beans

Preparation time: 10 minutes

Cooking time: 10 minutes

Overall time: 20 minutes

Serves: 4 to 6 people

Recipe Ingredients:

- 2 pounds of grass-fed ground beef
- 1 tablespoon of minced garlic
- 1 tablespoon of avocado oil
- 1 onion, diced
- 1 green pepper, diced
- 1 tablespoon of salt
- 1 tablespoon of smoked paprika
- ¼ teaspoon of cayenne pepper
- 3 tablespoons of chili powder
- 1 tablespoon of cumin
- 21 ounces of fire roasted diced tomatoes (1.5 cans)
- 2 tablespoons of tomato paste
- 4 ounces of can green chilies
- Juice from 1 lime
- 3 bay leaves

Cooking Instructions:

1. Set Ninja Foodi to Saute function, medium-high heat.

2. and add diced onion, green pepper, and avocado oil and saute for about 2 minutes. Add ground beef, salt, smoked paprika, cayenne pepper, chili powder, and cumin.

3. Stir and sauté until ground beef is browned Drain canned tomatoes and add to the pot along with the green chilies, tomato paste, and lime juice.

4. Stir until well combined. Add bay leaves, put the pressure cooker lid on and pressure cook on high for about 10 minutes

5. Once it finishes cooking let it sit for about 5 minutes to relieve the pressure. After 5 minutes flip the vent knob over to vent, let all the steam vent out.

6. Remove the lid, give it a good stir and serve. Serve with your favorite toppings.

Pulled Pork

Preparation time: 3 minutes

Cooking time: 2 hours 10 minutes

Overall time: 2 hours 13 minutes

Serves: 4 to 6 people

Recipe Ingredients:

- 3 pounds of boneless pork roast, frozen or fresh
- 1 cup of chicken bone broth
- 2 teaspoons of natural ancient sea salt
- 1 teaspoon of black pepper
- 1 teaspoon of smoked paprika
- 1 teaspoon of garlic powder
- ½ teaspoon of red pepper flakes
- ¾ cup of sugar-free barbeque sauce

Cooking Instructions:

1. Add the frozen or fresh roast, bone broth and seasonings to the removable cooking pot.

2. Close the Pressure Lid, turn the valve to Sealing position and set the Ninja Foodi to Pressure Cook.

3. It will take about 10 minutes to come to pressure since the meat is frozen. If you're using fresh meat, then it will come to pressure sooner.

4. Set the time to 90 minutes and press the Start/Stop button. Set the valve to Venting position for a quick release of the air.

5. Once the steam finishes escaping. Open the pressure lid. Remove the roast from the pressure cooker and shred the meat with meat claws or two forks.

6. Turn the Ninja Foodi to "Sear/Sauté" and allow the cooking broth to come to a rolling boil/bubble.

7. Mix in the BBQ sauce and allow it to reduce by half (~5 minutes). Mix in the shredded meat to the cooker and turn the Ninja Foodi off.

Beef Bacon Cabbage Casserole

Preparation time: 5 minutes

Cooking time: 5 minutes

Overall time: 10 minutes

Serves: 2 to 4 people

Recipe Ingredients:

- 1 pound of ground sirloin or beef
- 4 ounces of Sour cream
- ½ head of cabbage
- 1 tablespoon. of paprika
- 1 cube of beef bouillon
- 3 strips of bacon
- 7 slices of provolone cheese

Cooking Instructions:

1. Set pot on sauté mode and add ground beef/sirloin.

2. Sauté for a minute. Cut bacon into 1 inch pieces, add paprika to pot along with beef and bacon.

3. Sauté all until lightly brown. Add one cup of water and cube of beef bouillon to pot. Let simmer for about one minute. Be sure you are not scolding the bottom.

4. Add sour cream and mix well. Cut your half of cabbage head and add on top of combination.

5. Set pot to High Pressure for about 3 minutes, then do a quick release. Add cheese on top and lower crisping lid.

6. Set to broil for 5 minutes until bubbly and brown. ENJOY!

Ninja Chili

Preparation time: 20 minutes

Cooking time: 10 minutes

Overall time: 30 minutes

Serves: 2 to 4 people

Recipe Ingredients:

- 2 tsp. of extra virgin olive oil
- 1 pound of steak
- 1 pound of ground beef
- 1/2 medium onion, chopped
- 1 medium/large green bell pepper, chopped
- 3 garlic cloves, minced
- 1 cup of cherry tomatoes, halved
- 2 tbsp. of tomato paste
- 1 tbsp. of chili powder
- 1 tsp. of cumin
- 1 tsp. salt
- 2 cups of chicken or bone broth

Cooking Instructions:

1. Set the Ninja Foodi function to sear/sauté and add olive oil.

2. Cut up the steak into small bite size pieces, add the steak to the Foodi and brown on all sides. While the steak is cooking, start prepping the veggies.

3. Chop the bell peppers and onions, mince the garlic. When the steak is browned, add the ground beef and brown.

4. Drain any excess grease. add the onion, bell pepper and garlic and cook for a few minutes until onions are soft and translucent.

5. While the veggies are cooking, prepare the tomatoes by cutting them in half. Stir in seasonings, tomato paste, halved cherry tomatoes, and bone broth.

6. Bring to a boil and then switch the Foodi function to pressure. Add the pressure cooking lid and switch the vent to seal.

7. Change the time to 10 minutes and select the start button. When the pressure cook time is finished, quick release the pressure by switching the valve to vent.

8. When the pressure has been released, carefully remove the lid. Serve the chili with your favorite low carb / keto toppings. Jalapeno slices, shredded cheddar cheese, and sour cream are great options.

Korean Pork Sticky Ribs

Preparation time: 15 minutes

Cooking time: 40 minutes

Overall time: 55 minutes

Serves: 2 to 4 people

Recipe Ingredients:

- 1 rack of ribs
- Green onions, chopped
- Sesame seeds

Dry Rub Ingredients:

- 2 teaspoons of garlic powder
- ½ tablespoon to red pepper flakes
- 1 tablespoon of black pepper
- ½ teaspoon of ginger
- 1 teaspoon of white pepper

Sauce Ingredients:

- ¼ cup of amino acids
- ¼ cup of Lakanto Sweetener Golden
- 1 teaspoon of sesame oil
- 1 teaspoon of True Lemon Crystallized orange ginger seasoning

Cooking Instructions:

1. Wash the ribs and remove the membrane off the back of them and pat dry with a paper towel.

2. In a bowl add dry rub ingredients, mix together and rub it on both sides of the meat. Add ½ cup of water to Ninja Foodi or Pressure Cooker.

3. Cut the ribs into thirds and place ribs vertically. Cook on pressure cooker for about 30 minutes. In a separate bowl add sauce ingredients and whisk together.

4. When the ribs are done allow 5 minutes of cooling and then release the pressure valve.

5. Remove ribs and apply sauce with brush to bottom of ribs first, place in a glass casserole dish and then brush with sauce on the top and sides.

6. Place oven rack 2nd from the top and broil on high for 3 to 5 minutes on each side. Remove ribs from oven and garnish with sesame seeds and chopped green onions.

Roasted Spaghetti Squash

Preparation time 5 minutes

Cooking time: 15 minutes

Overall time 20 minutes

Serves: 4 to 6 people

Recipe Ingredients:

- 1 large spaghetti squash, (cut in half lengthwise)
- 1 cup of water
- 2 tomatoes, (diced)
- 2 tablespoons of parsley, (chopped)
- 1 ¼ teaspoon Italian seasoning, (dried)
- 1 tablespoon of olive oil
- 6 of pieces of bacon, (chopped)
- As desired salt and pepper
- 2 cup of parmesan cheese, (grated)
- 1 cup of mozzarella cheese, shredded

Cooking Instructions:

1. Place the water in the Foodi bowl. Place the trivet in the bowl and place the squash halves on the trivet.

2. Place the lid on and set to sealing position. Cook on pressure cook for about 8 minutes.

3. Open the lid away from you and carefully remove the squash by using the trivet to bring it out of the bowl.

4. With a spoon, remove the seeds and center matter from both halves. Then, with a fork, begin to scratch away the spaghetti strands and place them into a bowl.

5. Add the parmesan cheese, ¾ of the cooked bacon, and 1 teaspoon of the Italian seasoning, and salt and pepper to bowl and mix well.

6. Working one half at a time, place the squash on the trivet and fill with half the contents from the bowl.

7. Top the squash with half the mozzarella cheese. Cover with the crisping lid and broil for about 5 minutes or until the cheese is melted and brown.

8. Repeat with the second half of the squash. while the squash is browning, in a small bowl, combine the diced tomatoes, remaining bacon, olive oil, 1/4 tsp of Italian seasoning and parsley.

9. When the squash is finished browning and you're ready to serve, divide the tomato mixture between each squash and spread over the top. Serve and enjoy!

Acknowledgement

In preparing the " Ultimate Ninja Foodi Cookbook", I sincerely wish to acknowledge my indebtedness to my husband for his support and the wholehearted cooperation and vast experience of my two colleagues - Mrs. Carol Newman and Mrs. Emily Cook.

Alexander Peterson

CPSIA information can be obtained
at www.ICGtesting.com
Printed in the USA
LVHW051011131120
671376LV00006B/351